The Story of Submarines

illustrated with photographs

Landmark
BOOKS

Random House New York

THE STORY
OF SUBMARINES

by George Weller

578

The author wishes to express his gratitude to these persons
for guidance, criticism and comment:
Frank J. Anderson, former director of the
Submarine Library, General Dynamics Corp.
Admiral George W. Anderson, Jr., chief of
naval operations
Rear Admiral E. M. Eller, chief of naval history
Captain John B. Hess
Lieutenant Commander Adam P. Kulik
Captain Hugh H. Lewis
Admiral Charles A. Lockwood, Jr.
Captain F. Kent Loomis
Lieutenant Patrick McKenna
Vice Admiral Chester C. Smith
Lieutenant Donald M. Ulmer
Rear Admiral Frederick B. Warder

CONTENTS

The Story of Submarines

1. A SUBMARINE HUNTS, STRIKES, AND ESCAPES

It is the final year of World War II. Somewhere in the Pacific a United States submarine is prowling the sea, seeking an enemy to sink. The officer of the deck and a quartermaster stand on her bridge, binoculars at their eyes. Above them on the platform on either side of the periscope shears, two more sailors scan the horizon. Behind them the radar antenna turns round and round, sweeping the horizon with its electronic eye.

Down below, the captain pauses to glance at the "Christmas tree" in the control room. This panel of tiny red and green lights tells him the condition, open or closed, of the openings in the hull, flood valves and vents of tanks. These openings admit sea water and make the submarine heavy enough to submerge. Across the room are the air valves that "blow out" the water and make the submarine light enough to travel on the surface.

Suddenly a loud-speaker barks: "Captain to the bridge!" The captain pauses by the radar operator as he goes up through the conning tower. "What's up?" he asks.

The operator answers, "Contact, captain. Bearing three-one-five, range 25,000 yards."

"Get me course and speed," the captain orders.

"Yes, sir—estimate course zero-one-two, speed ten knots."

The captain leaps for the ladder, climbs up and emerges on the bridge. He speaks quietly to his officer of the deck (O.O.D.), who broadcasts through the loud-speaker: "Maneuvering bridge. Answer bells on four main engines." To the helmsman the O.O.D. shouts, "All ahead full; come right to new course zero-one-two."

The powerful Diesel engines throb with increased power. The dim white wave at the bow climbs higher. The chase has begun.

On the bridge the O.O.D., the quartermaster and the captain, as well as the lookouts at the periscope shears above them, are straining to sight a ship's smoke against the horizon. The loud-speaker makes the only sound heard above the deep monotone of the engines. Over it the radar operator calmly reports the shortening ranges to the enemy's ships.

Inside the conning tower a "plotting party" is trying to figure what speed and exact course their enemy is making.

The captain slides down the ladder for a quick peep at the radar screen. Greenish lighted "pips" now show on the screen. These represent one big and several little ships zigzagging in and out. A screen of destroyers is apparently changing direction to make tracking and attack difficult. They must be protecting something bigger— perhaps a cargo ship or a fat tanker.

When the captain comes up to the bridge again, the ships are in view.

At 21,000 yards the captain orders the attacking course. He plans to overtake and pass the ships, so he can place his submarine directly in the convoy's path. But as he speeds past the unseeing destroyers and ahead, the captain stays well out of their range of vision. He is taking no chances.

In the conning tower, sailors of the plotting party cluster around the torpedo data computer (TDC), the mechanical brains of the attack. They crank information into its maze of whirling dials and flashing lights. "Range 20,000 . . . set, bearing two-six-oh . . . set, angle on the bow, starboard six-five . . . set."

Timing the zigzags of the biggest and fastest ships, the captain tries to guess the dodging plan of the convoy's commander. Soon the submarine reaches the "diving point," ten miles ahead of the onrushing ships.

Turning toward the loud-speaker the captain says: "Take her down!"

The piercing *aaaa-oooo-gaaa, aaaa-oooo-gaaa* of the diving alarm reverberates throughout the ship.

"Clear the bridge!" shouts the O.O.D. above. Down the hatch slide the lookouts and the O.O.D., excited but steady. They are riding almost on each other's shoulders.

With the roar of water rushing into the ballast tanks, the submarine slips cleanly under. The speed drops away from 18 to 5 knots.

A few feet below the waves the captain orders the approach periscope hoisted from its well for a long-distance look at the oncoming enemy. Pressing his face against the rubber-cushioned eyepiece, the captain cautiously rotates the periscope through a full circle to see that no ships are close by.

Then he settles on the convoy. "Bearing . . . mark! Range . . . mark!" A quartermaster notes the bearing on a dial above his head.

"Down 'scope," the captain says, snapping the periscope's handles into position with a metallic click. Down slides the periscope below the waves. The submarine is invisible. The whole operation has taken less than 15 seconds.

"Angle on the bow, starboard ten," announces the captain. "Target is a heavy tanker escorted by three destroyers. We'll have to get past those three 'cans.' Rig ship for silent running."

Sailors leap to shut off fans, electric motors, air-conditioning machines. The automatic machinery is now worked quietly by hand. The sailors slip off their shoes and move about only as necessary in order to make as little noise as possible.

The sound man, muffled in the heavy earphones of the sonar equipment, speaks up. "Contact, captain . . . bearing two-zero-two. Light, fast screws, with slow heavy screws in background. . . . No other contacts."

"Very well," says the captain. "Make ready all tubes forward. Set depth 10 feet, speed high. We'll fire 3 at the tanker, using 150 percent coverage. We'll save the others in case these three 'cans' bother us."

The captain is deliberately spreading the torpedoes like fingers on a hand. This will make up for any errors in figuring the tanker's course. It will also keep the target covered if the ship tries to dodge away. He sets the torpedoes at shallow depth so that, if a destroyer cuts across in front of the target, it will be hit.

The metal mind of the TDC also begins sending corrected angles directly into the torpedoes so that they will run true to the target no matter how the submarine changes course.

Submerged like this, the electronic eye of the radar is blind. The submarine cannot see electrically. And now the captain dares not order the sonarman to send out an echo-ranging ping to seek and locate the ship. The enemy destroyers could hear it and know an attack is imminent.

Only the eye of the periscope is left, with all the risks of lifting it above the waves. The captain elevates it, peers through. "Bearing . . . mark! . . . Masthead height 110 feet . . . mark."

"Set," says the TDC officer, cranking in the new information. "Range 4,000 yards," says the captain's periscope assistant. "Set," again, from the TDC.

"Here come the destroyers," says the captain. "See if we can get past 'em." He shouts to the diving officer: "Make your depth 150 feet." The waves close over the periscope. "Sonar, report anything suspicious."

Then comes the enemy's first sound: the chirp of his sonar, searching for them. A nervous hush fills the submarine. The chirps grow louder. Then comes the *shir-shir-shir* of a heavy destroyer's propellers. Closer . . . nearer . . . overhead . . . fading off astern.

"They missed us," says a voice. A sigh comes from every mouth. "Periscope depth," says the captain coolly, and the submarine noses up again.

"Up 'scope for a look around; put me on the destroyers." The periscope hisses up from its well, already facing the target. The captain snaps down the handles and whirls the steel pole to the destroyer's bearing. The captain's smile, as he looks through the eyepiece, reassures the fire-control party watching his expression. Another peek, this time at the tanker. She is only 1200 yards away and rushing blindly nearer.

A green light shows in the conning tower. A phone talker speaks up: "Bow tubes ready, captain."

"Very well. Open the outer doors." To his periscope assistant, the captain says, "Final bearing and shoot. Up 'scope!" Before the vertical eye breaks the waves, the captain is at the eyepiece. The excitement has tightened his voice. "Bearing . . . *mark* . . . no range. Down 'scope!"

The broad-bowed tanker is so close the captain almost hates to spend three torpedoes where one might kill. But he has worked too hard to risk missing. A quick glance at the destroyers going away, then back to the target.

"Stand by, forward! Sonar, track each fish. Fire one."

"Set!" shouts the TDC operator. His assistant pushes his palm on the big firing button.

A heavy cough of air and a push as the first torpedo kicks away. Four seconds, six, eight—and away goes the second "fish" with a hiss of farewell. Eight more seconds and the third is off— racing at more than forty miles an hour. But where?

Everyone listens tensely. The sonarman speaks

up: "All torpedoes running hot, straight and normal."

"Very well," says the captain. "Now put me onto the destroyers. They'll be back soon. Up 'scope!" But before the periscope breaks the surface a deep *groomph* causes the sub's hull to shudder. A cheer breaks out.

"Got him!"

His eye to the periscope, the captain watches the flames leap up on the stricken ship. "Good hit," he says quietly.

The crew counts seconds. Eight seconds pass— no further sound. Number two must have missed. Another eight seconds go by—then *gaarroomph!* "A big tanker, all right," says the captain, peering again. "Faster than we figured."

The sonar operator speaks up urgently: "Destroyer bearing zero-two-five, speeding up and turning this way."

"Here he comes!" says the captain. "Get me down! Three hundred feet and rig for depth charges! Estimate range 2500 yards."

He swings his periscope around for a last glance before the waves smother it. Over the tanker's broken hull, sheets of orange flame climb toward the sky. Running men, tiny shadows against the light, throw themselves over the rails, preferring a sleepy death in the icy water to being roasted alive.

The periscope, submerged and blind, is lowered again. The long metal body of the submarine angles heavily downward. The deck tilts. The men steady themselves. They, the hunters, are now being hunted. Down! Down!

The sonar operator warns that the destroyer is tearing dead at them, ready to attack. The crewmen glance quickly around the submarine's interior, looking for anything loose. They even grab their tools lest they fall on the deck and make a giveaway noise.

The needle of the depth gauge goes around with painful slowness—down, down, 120 feet, 140. Now the crew can hear the *shum-shum* of the pursuing propellers above, drawing near at three times the submarine's speed of escape. Only depth and a swift, tricky turn of course can save them. So they plunge deeper. But there is a limit. They dare not go too deep, or the sea's strong, cold arms will crush the thin submarine.

"Level her off," orders the captain. "Rig for

silent running." To run quietly and save battery power, the submarine slows to two knots.

Carefully the captain turns his creeping submarine away from the chasing, listening destroyer. By turning, his submarine presents only a narrow width of hull to reflect the searching sound waves of the enemy sonar and reveal its presence.

"Passing overhead," says the sonar operator in a level voice. The attack is coming.

The *schir-schir-schir* sound of the hated screws prickles the scalps of the tense men. The sonar operator, figuring his position, says: "I think he's dropped the first one."

"Right, full rudder," orders the captain. "New course one-three-five." He hopes, by this last-minute twist, to escape the deadly lacework of depth charges to come.

Each man imagines the depth charges being flung outward from the destroyer's fantail. The ash cans are coming down, down, down . . .

Crack! Whoom! Whish! Whush! The men are flung against the bulkheads. Some are knocked sprawling on the decks. The whole boat shudders around them. *Crack! Whoom! Whish! Whush!* A shower of broken light bulbs and indicator dials tinkles down onto the deck and into the bilges. The only light left is the dimmed glow of the battle lanterns.

The crew hears four separate sounds with each depth charge. First there is the *crack* of the sound wave, then the *whoom* as the whole submarine shudders and pushes downward. Next comes the *whish* of water expelled from the tanks in the outer shell of the submarine, followed by the *whush* of the same water going back to fill the vacuum caused by the explosion.

The reliable murmur of the slowed motors stammers and stops. The submarine hangs motionless. Her fins, the hydroplanes, are useless with no headway. The crew, too, is frozen by fear. Nobody moves. Is death coming? How can they hide?

One chance remains: to get the submarine under a stiff layer of colder water. Cold water, being denser, can deflect the probing fingers of the enemy's sonar waves. The crew's lives now depend on the skill of one man: the diving officer.

Down . . . down . . . down . . . past the limits of the submarine's bulkheads. The steel walls weep and leak. But they hold.

Again the depth charges explode. Again the men fall, but with skinned elbows and wrenched knees they struggle to their feet. They are under the cold layer now, in the cellar of the sea. The nervous chirp of the destroyer's sonar vanishes. But are they saved?

"Fire!" someone shouts. "Fire in the maneuvering room!" An evil smell of smoke drifts through their narrow chamber.

The captain snaps: "Clear the maneuvering room and secure it. Damage control party lay aft on the double." The men in the damage control party don smoke masks, while the rest of the crew strap on oxygen-breathing apparatus. The smoke is poisoning the air they breathe. Shirts are soaked with perspiration. Breaths get shorter.

The pressure hull has been dished in. The hull is leaking at the seams. The new danger is that the extra weight of the intruding sea will drag them down deeper, below "collapse depth."

To pump or not to pump? The pump's heavy noise might reach the ears above. But the captain hopes the sizzling columns of bubbles from the depth charges will drown out the rhythmic groan of the pumps. He orders them started, to remove water from the auxiliary ballast tanks and keep trim.

Crack! Whoom! whish! whush!—again and again the depth charges explode.

The damage control party, wearing breathing apparatus, undo the door to the maneuvering room and plunge in. They find that the fire started with a short circuit of wires broken by the shock of depth charges. The cork inner lining of the hull is burning. The flames have spread to rags. The interior is oily blue with smoke. The fire fighters smother the flames with carbon dioxide, not water, so the electrical equipment won't be damaged. Twice the door opens and the men stagger out to fall gasping on the engine-room gratings.

"Pass in more extinguishers." Two men wearing rescue breathing apparatus take them in. ·

The sonar operator speaks, a little shaky now. "Screws bearing three-zero-six, closing. I think he's making another run." The word spreads like poisoned smoke through the hull. To himself the captain murmurs, "We can never take another string of charges." But each man stays at his station, hands on his controls. Their lives depend on these last few seconds. Will their long months of training save them? Perhaps.

The submarine feels still, heavy and lifeless, like a great dead fish. Everyone waits.

Then the sonar operator speaks up, cautious but clear. "Contact now drawing left . . . getting weaker, too. He's shifting to long-scale pinging. . . . I think he lost us, captain."

"Thank God," says someone. "He's gone."

"Could be, but stay with him," the captain tells the sonar operator.

Looking around, everyone notices more leaks. The destroyer has gone, but the sea is still trying to drag them down. A repair party starts calking seams, tightening glands, shutting off valves.

Now there comes a new, strange sound through the water. At first it sounds like metallic wrapping paper being crumpled. What new terror is this? The sonar operator relieves them again: "Tanker sinking, sir. I can hear breaking-up noises."

All around the submarine there is heard a gobbling, a gurgling, a bubbling. It is the sound of the merciless sea, forcing itself into the enemy tanker. It is creeping into the places where enemy sailors once lived—into their bunks and cabins, their chairs, books, lockers, their engine rooms, their wardrooms and toilets. The submarine crew hears this sound, the exultant sound the sea makes when throttling a ship.

Nobody moves. If one of those depth charges had been twenty feet nearer—

The door of the maneuvering room bursts open with a clang. "Fire extinguished, sir," says a fire-blackened lieutenant, staggering out.

"Well done, men," says the captain. The motors are coaxed back to life. The stern is swung toward the departing destroyers.

Already it is 10:00 P.M. These night hours are precious. Only in darkness does a submarine dare come up and breathe. Below, the temperature is 125 degrees. Men drink, sweat, and wipe themselves with towels. Even the deck is slippery with the nasty dew of condensation. To relieve the heavy air, soda lime, an absorbent for carbon dioxide, is spread on mattresses. Some men are trembling, running a fever caused by tension. Nearly all have headaches.

"If only we could start the air-conditioners!" whispers one man. But every spurt of battery current is needed for the motors. The captain, in

sneakers, moves from compartment to compartment, encouraging his men. He has put on his
red goggles, both to protect his eyes for night
vision later and to demonstrate to the crew that
he hopes to surface soon.

The submarine creeps up through the cold roof
of water and listens. No sonar pings.

"Up periscope." Are the glass optics of the
periscope broken? No, they have survived.

At a sixty-five-foot depth, the captain sweeps
the horizon. Nothing. Now up to a forty-seven-
foot depth, where the dish of the radar emerges.
Still safe.

Three blasts on the klaxon, and the boat
surfaces.

"Open the hatch," orders the captain.

The conning-tower hatch, leading to the bridge
above, is undogged. At first the compressed air,
foul with smoke, rushes out. The lookout party
scrambles up. The Diesel engines throb into life.
Soon they will be able to restore the batteries.
Now sweet fresh air is sucked down.

Standing on shaky legs on his dripping bridge,
the captain strips off his goggles, rakes the black
horizon with his binoculars, and talks into the

speaker again. "All hands, this is the captain speaking. We've come through once more, thanks to your good work. Congratulations and well done. Damage control party, keep after those leaks. Secure from battle stations. In one hour we submerge. We hope all hands can get a well-deserved rest. Set the watch. Course zero-nine-oh."

He turns to the lookouts. "Remember, we're still in enemy waters. Let's return very cautiously and search the area. Keep a sharp lookout."

At his desk, later, with a cup of coffee in his hand, he starts to write a patrol report. His executive officer knocks on his bulkhead.

"Fished this up just now. Must be theirs, sir." It is a life ring, with the name of the dead ship.

"Did you look her up in the registry?"

"Yes, sir—tanker, 17,000 tons."

"Better turn in and get some sleep."

The captain's mind goes briefly to the enemy ship, shattered, crushed, sleeping forever below. Then he resumes writing his report.

2. THE SUBMARINE IS BORN

Today's submarines are such scientific marvels they seem to belong exclusively to the twentieth century. But the first reports of attempts to navigate under water go back many centuries. One of the ancient Greek historians mentions that some of Alexander the Great's soldiers used diving bells for attacking under water. And in 320 B.C. Alexander himself is supposed to have descended into the water in some kind of primitive glass barrel. It may have been a wooden barrel equipped with glass ports. His purpose was to observe the fish and other undersea life.

The principle behind the early diving bell was a simple one. Sometime after cups came into use, man noticed a strange thing. If he forced his cup into water upside down, it didn't fill. The air stayed in. The water stayed out. The cup became a chamber of air *under water*. Why couldn't a huge cupful of air, with a man inside, be lowered into the sea?

And so the diving bell was born, perhaps a thousand years before the Christian era. This diving bell was suspended from a boat by a rope.

After the British navy sank Spain's vast armada of ships in A.D. 1588, English divers rode down in iron chambers to recover heavy cannon. Each diver, sitting in his little chamber of air, dared not venture outside. He had to work fast and breathe slow, making his tiny closetful of air last till his own breath fouled it. The diving bell was a "submarine," in that it went "under the water," as the word means. But its motion was only up and down like an elevator.

Probably the first submariner to travel horizontally under water was a secretive Dutch engineer named Cornelis Drebbel. Drebbel got the idea of a submarine by watching fishing boats on the Thames. He noticed that they plunged low when pulling heavy baskets of fish in the water behind them. But they rose quickly when the baskets were released. With more power pulling forward, and plenty of weight, he felt that a boat could be nosed right under the waves.

In 1620, at about the same time the Pilgrims were sailing for the New World, Drebbel built a submarine on the Thames River in London. The submarine was made from grease-soaked leather stretched on a wooden frame. Twelve oars stuck out through holes in the waterproof leather. And twelve husky men sat inside the hot little craft and rowed. But no matter how heartily the oarsmen pulled, the cautious inventor never could plunge deeper than twelve or fifteen feet.

There were other early attempts to construct an underwater craft, but the first fighting submarine didn't appear until 1776. David Bushnell, while a student at Yale, built it for the American rebels. He dreamed that his *Turtle* would single-handedly scatter the British fleet, solving all of General George Washington's problems.

To push his egg-shaped little submarine through the water, Bushnell used a kind of crude propeller. This propeller, or "oar" as he called it, was "formed upon the principle of the screw. Its axis entered the vessel, and being turned one way rowed the vessel [forward], but being turned the other way rowed it backward; it was made to be turned by hand or foot. At the top there was likewise an oar [propeller] for ascending or descending or continuing at any particular depth."

The keel consisted of 700 pounds of lead. Two hundred pounds of this could be cast off from inside in case of emergency. This would allow the lightened *Turtle* to rise to the surface. There was room in the submarine for just one man sitting upright. In addition to cranking the propellers, he steered by means of a rudder and peered through portholes placed in a kind of conning tower at the top of the craft.

The *Turtle* also had ballast tanks which could be filled with sea water by means of hand pumps. This made the submarine heavy enough to sink. When the operator wished to rise to the surface, he used the pumps to empty the tanks. The hull was formed of oak planking bent into shape, held together with iron bands and smeared over with tar to prevent leaks. The little craft looked rather like two tortoise shells joined together.

On the evening of September 6, 1776, the guns of the anchored British man-of-war *Eagle* glowered over New York Bay, blockading it. Sergeant Ezra Lee, a volunteer submariner from Old Lyme, Connecticut, squeezed himself into the *Turtle*. Cranking his "oar," he set out alone to sink the monster anchored in the bay. The daring sergeant was carrying with him a 150-pound charge of powder, the world's first torpedo. It was fastened to the outside of the hull, and a rope tied to the gunpowder-filled torpedo was attached to a screw which could be turned from inside the submarine. The primitive torpedo also had a kind of timer or clock fuse. The sergeant was to screw the torpedo rope to the wooden bottom of the British *Eagle*, start the clockwork of the timer, and back off to escape the explosion. For all of these tasks, he had just enough air to last him thirty minutes.

At about 3:00 A.M. the *Turtle* crept under the sleeping *Eagle*. But when Lee tried to carry out his assignment he found that the screw wouldn't penetrate the metal-sheathed hull of the British ship. In attempting to move to another place, he lost touch with the *Eagle*. Despite this mishap he turned loose the torpedo in the open sea. The clockwork went perfectly, and the charge exploded. The British, seeing the geyser of water, thought they were being shelled. They moved their ships farther downstream.

The *Turtle* made two more attempts but each time she was tricked by the swift Hudson River tide. The British, angry at the submarine's impudence, pursued the *Turtle's* mother ship while the submarine was on deck, and sank them both.

Washington later said: "I then thought and still think it was an effort of genius, but that too many things were necessary to be combined . . . against an enemy who are always upon guard."

Almost a quarter of a century later, another American, Robert Fulton, turned his attention to the problems of underwater travel. In 1797, while a student in Paris, he began drawing up plans for a submarine called the *Nautilus*. By 1800 she was practically completed. The vessel was daringly built with a long hull shaped like a cucumber. Near the bow was a tower with a glass eye where the inventor "conned" or steered. This was the first real conning tower.

For underwater power Fulton adapted Bushnell's hand-turned propeller. The *Nautilus* was twenty-one feet, four inches long and about seven feet across. Iron ribs held her wooden planks together. Her hull was covered with copper sheets. There were valves which opened to flood the tanks when the craft submerged. But Fulton used the principle of compressed air instead of hand pumps to force the water out of the tanks when the time came to surface. The plunging boat could disguise herself as a fisherman's trawler when on the surface of the water, for she carried a collapsible mast on which to rig a real sail.

Napoleon Bonaparte gave Fulton funds to help build the *Nautilus*. France was then at war with Great Britain. Napoleon, first consul of the new French Republic, wanted a blockade smasher to frighten away the British fleet. One day in May, 1801, he stood on the weedy quay of the River Seine, arms folded, to watch the *Nautilus* dive. First Fulton, with a crewman to help him, took the submarine down to twenty-five feet. They stayed there twenty minutes, watching their gauges by candlelight, while the stream took them three miles toward the sea. Then, cranking manfully, they emerged and came upstream at a speed of two knots. Napoleon was impressed and requested a test at sea.

Fulton put glass bull's-eyes in his deck for light, so that he would not have candles using up his air. Then, in the harbor of Brest, he went down to a depth of twenty-three feet. He stayed there for some time, poking around the bottom of the harbor with three sailors. Napoleon grew more interested. Perhaps the English Channel could become French.

But Fulton attached several conditions to selling the submarine to France. He wanted a bonus: "4,000 francs for every English ship above forty guns which the inventor destroys." He was worried about the French turning against the United States. "Being a citizen of the United States, I desire it to be stipulated that this invention or a similar one will not be used by the French government against the United States." He was worried also about his neck. Sailors who launched fire ships against anchored vessels were hanged. He insisted that his crew were to be treated as prisoners of war, "and any hurt done to them . . . to be met by similar reprisals on English prisoners."

An old schooner, anchored off Brest, became a demonstration target. *Nautilus*, with Fulton at the controls, approached her, submerged. Fulton fixed his twenty-pound torpedo and blew her to pieces. (He called his underwater explosive a "torpedo" after the electric ray or crampfish—a member of the family *Torpedinidae*—which shocks its prey to death.)

Napoleon was impressed by the demonstration, but his admirals were not. They thought Fulton's submarine could never "help the French scatter terror before their invasion of England," as he had promised. His back-breaking, hand-cranked propeller could never take the place of strong wind on stout canvas. Moreover, Napoleon's admirals decided it was ungentlemanly for submarines to sink ships without giving them a chance to shoot back. One of the officers wrote, "This type of warfare carries with it an objection: those who undertake it, and also those against whom it is launched, will all perish. And this cannot be called a gallant death."

When the French finally rejected his invention, Fulton went across the Channel to England. There the British Prime Minister, William Pitt, always sympathetic toward Americans, befriended the Yankee inventor. Fulton was given funds with which to start building a submarine. When the new boat was finished, Fulton blew an old brig in halves with 170 pounds of gunpowder. But the British admirals thought the Prime Minister was a dreamer. "Pitt," wrote one scornful admiral, "is the greatest fool who ever existed, to encourage a mode of warfare that those who command the seas do not want and which, if successful, would deprive them of it." Another naval officer said if that "gimcrack" were adopted by the fleet, it would end by doing away with the navy.

Disgusted, Fulton returned to America, where Congress gave him $5,000 to develop his experiments. He was supposed to blow up a ship, but this time it was the United States Navy that foiled him. The target ship was draped so thoroughly by nets hung on spars that Fulton couldn't penetrate the thick curtain to set off his charge.

The inventor then went on to make the first commercially successful paddle steamer. But the steamer could never push the submarine out of his head. "I will not admit that it [the steamer] is half so important as the torpedo system of defence or attack," he wrote.

Fulton spent the profits from his steamboat monopoly building a huge armored submarine, eighty feet long and fourteen feet deep. It was fitted with underwater guns. He called it the *Mute* because it would attack silently. *Mute* could carry a colossal crew of ninety men, but she never went to sea. Fulton died before she could be launched.

3. THE SUBMARINE GOES TO WAR

After Fulton several other inventors and adventurers tried their hand at building a successful underwater vessel in both America and Europe. But not until the fourth year of the American Civil War was there any really dramatic development.

In the South, the Confederate States found themselves in the ever tightening grip of a Union naval blockade. Shipments of guns and other armaments were cut off, and along the Southern seaboard the wharves were stacked high with cotton. The bales could not be shipped to Europe because of the Northern warships waiting outside the harbors. A workable submarine could destroy the blockade, release the cotton, and open the door to imports. It would thus provide a source of money and supplies for the South, rich in cotton but poor in factories.

At Charleston, South Carolina, an inventor named Theodore Stoney designed a kind of small torpedo boat. She was cut as close to the water as possible with only a few inches of the hull showing. And the top was covered with iron plating. The little boat was called the *David*. Her mission was to bring down the giant warships anchored offshore just as the Biblical David felled the giant Goliath.

The *David* was about thirty feet long and sixty-six inches wide. Painted a dull gray, she was driven by a steam engine with a two-bladed propeller. The little boat couldn't fully submerge, because her little boiler had to breathe. But she sped along at eye-level depth at a swift seven knots. The *David's* slingshot was a fifteen-foot hollow spar protruding from her nose like a long spear. A sixty-pound can of blasting powder was mounted on this spar.

The *David* was supposed to ram her enemy, jabbing in the spar like a bee's stinger. The shock would set off a tricky chain of seven chemical fuses inside the lance. But *David*, unlike a bee, was supposed to hang on, not fly away. Stoney, the inventor, hoped that the little boat would not be blown up by the force of the explosion.

"Operating *David*," wrote a French war reporter, "was quite perilous and required a crew who were select, alert and rugged."

Lieutenant W. T. Glassell and a crew of three volunteers steered *David* downstream on the misty night of October 5, 1863. They planned to surprise the *New Ironsides*, an armored steam sloop anchored in blockade off Charleston Harbor. Silently they slipped past Fort Sumter. Then the Union sloop loomed in the dark. While the sweating crew stoked the boiler fire like fiends, the *David* crept near.

Suddenly Ensign C. W. Howard, the sloop's officer on deck watch, saw the torpedo boat's dark form slithering closer. "Ahoy, there!" he shouted.

Glassell poked a rifle out of his conning tower, aimed, and pressed the trigger. Howard fell dead.

As the Northern sailors peppered the conning tower with bullets, Glassell stabbed the long, chemical-plugged lance of *David* into the sloop. His sweating crewmen cowered below, waiting for the blast to tear them apart or set them free. Instead, when the sixty-pound charge blew, it only threw a geyser of water onto the sloop's deck. But the watery explosion also flooded

David's open conning tower. Her boilers were drowned in sea water. Without power the little boat floundered helplessly in the water.

"All hands abandon ship!" cried Glassell, diving overboard. He was picked up, swimming, by a Union coal schooner. His fireman, hanging like a barnacle to the sloop's anchor chain, tried to surrender, but in the confusion no one heard him. Flooded, the *David* drifted away, bullets dancing off her iron plating. Then came the kind of miracle that sometimes saves submarines. The remaining crew members—including one engineer who couldn't swim—somehow got a fire going under the hissing boilers. Scared, blackened and confused, they brought the *David* home.

The Northerners were shocked. *New Ironsides* wore nearly five inches of armor over her 27-inch-thick timbers. The blast from the *David* had only opened a bulkhead and blown some sailors off their feet. But where would *David* strike next? A telegram from Washington warned the Union admiral that "the rebels have a plan to blow up the fleet."

On Union ships day and night watches were doubled, making blockading a nervous, sleepless job instead of a sailor's nap. Boilers were kept heated up to full pressure for emergency departure. Coal was wasted while the ships sat still. Bunkers ran low. Booms were rigged all around the warships with nets hanging from them, till the men-of-war looked ridiculously like ladies with veils.

The Confederates built other David-type boats. But after the attack on *New Ironsides* the Northern ships were on the alert. Something better than a torpedo boat was needed. This time the Southerners tried a real submarine.

Early in 1862 two Southern army captains and a civilian engineer had built a submarine at New Orleans. But before the boat saw any action, Union forces captured New Orleans. The submarine was scuttled to prevent its falling into Union hands, and the builders escaped to Mobile, Alabama. There they built a second underwater craft. Plans were drawn up for this one to attack the Northern fleet, but it plunged to the bottom of Mobile Bay when a sudden storm blew up.

At this point Captain H. L. Hunley, one of the builders of the two earlier submarines, put up the necessary funds for a third try. The C.S.S. *Hunley*, as the new submarine was later named, went back to the idea of a propeller driven by a crank shaft painfully turned by hard-breathing seamen. Designed by James McClintock, the craft was about thirty feet long and four feet wide. At each end there were compartments containing tanks which could be flooded by valves or pumped dry by hand pumps. Iron weights were hung outside the hull as extra ballast. These could be dropped off if the submarine needed to rise in a hurry.

On *Hunley's* first dive, the flames of her railroad lanterns flickered low after only a half-hour. It was a question if the lamps didn't use up more oxygen than the crew. On the next trip the submarine stayed down five times as long, de-lighting her engineers.

Then came disaster. The submarine plunged down and stuck fast in the mud. By the time divers and tugs hauled her up, her volunteer crew had met a dry death in the arms of the sea—not drowned but suffocated. Every lantern, though still full of oil, had gone out for lack of oxygen.

In spite of the tragedy, the *Hunley* was hauled with great difficulty to Charleston. There Lieutenant John Payne of the Confederate Navy took command of the ill-fated vessel. One night, just as the *Hunley* was preparing to go out to attack, a big steamer swept by. The heavy waves from the steamer's wake washed over the *Hunley's* conning tower, which was open. Down she went. Only her captain escaped. He was climbing up the hatchway at the time and managed to get out.

The tragic hull was raised again, and the bodies of her unfortunate crew were removed. Who would volunteer to die in her on the next mission? Once more Lieutenant Payne took charge, and again she was swamped. Payne escaped death a second time, and he was also able to save two sailors. The others chalked their last farewells to their families on the wet iron walls.

The next time it was even more difficult to find anyone willing to take the diving coffin down. Finally Captain Horace L. Hunley, the man who had helped pay for the monster, agreed to take over. Again the volunteers shuffled timidly forward, their eyes bright with courage, fear and the fascination of the unknown. Hunley trained them carefully and checked the craft to make sure everything was working properly. Then he made a practice dive. The submarine went down too steeply, sticking her nose in the mud. Unloading the weights to lighten her was not enough to make her surface. By the time she was pulled up, Hunley and his crew were dead.

Regardless of drowned submariners, the struggle to break the Union blockade had to go on. Unless the Confederate States were successful, they could never sell their cotton for vitally needed munitions and supplies.

Lieutenant George A. Dixon, who had helped build the *Hunley*, next assumed command. He had full confidence in his submarine and enlisted as crew at least one artilleryman and nine suicidal seadogs. He was determined to attack a Northern warship somehow, and if he had to drown he was going to take some Yankees with him.

After three or four months of night patrols, Dixon selected as target the U.S.S. *Housatonic*, a Federal steam sloop which was unwisely anchored in the channel only two and a half miles from the inlet where the *Hunley* was stationed.

This time the Union navy was alert. From spies they already knew that the Charleston shipyards had a row of *Davids* waiting, and they had heard of the "Diver," as the Yankees called the *Hunley*. The *Housatonic*, with steam up to her engine throttles, was prepared for an attack.

Dixon and his men shook hands for the last time, crawled in, and cast off. Inside the long boiler tube where so many men had died, the artillery man and the nine sweating sailors cranked for their lives. In the darkness, at the conning tower, Dixon guided *Hunley* cautiously under the main battery of the blockading *Housatonic's* guns, so the muzzles could not be lowered to fire at the submarine.

Peering out of the conning tower—he had been forbidden to submerge—Dixon tried to force the *Hunley's* spar torpedo, carrying 90 pounds of explosive, into the *Housatonic's* side. He had chosen the right place: a touchy point forward of the mainmast and opposite the ship's powder magazine.

Shouts followed—roars of alarm, orders, boatswains' whistles, cries of pain—then rifle shots. The smoking *Housatonic*, her side torn open, sank into the moonlit water.

The submarine, the weapon of the new age, had scored her first kill.

But into the black darkness of the sea, her flank against the huge *Housatonic*, there sank another little hull. It was the final drowning for the *Hunley*, but at last the stubborn pigmy had imposed her will on a giant.

After blowing a hole in her enemy, the *Hunley* apparently failed to back off. She was dragged below, along with the wounded *Housatonic*.

4. THE SUBMARINE GROWS UP

The early submarine was a brave threat but a suicidal weapon. Too many men died in those first submarines. They died because the air supply quickly gave out and the power under water was too weak. The crews also died because they were unable to conquer gravity and lift the water-loaded hulls from the sea's floor. The sea was heavier than they, and pressed them down. After their compressed air was exhausted, they were unable to blow the heavy water out of the tanks and rise. The propellers were too feeble to pull the boats loose from a sticky bottom, free them from a trapped anchor, or help them escape an over-hanging rock.

To understand the problems of the early submarines, it is necessary to know something of the principles of buoyancy and water pressure. *Buoyancy* is the upward force or pressure which holds up a ship when it is in the water. If the ship floats on the water surface it has what is called *positive* buoyancy. If it sinks it has *negative* buoyancy; that is, it has *no* buoyancy to hold it up.

Even when a ship floats, some of its hull has to be in the water. And the part that is below the surface pushes aside, or displaces, some of the water. If the displaced water could be collected and weighed, that weight would be what is known as the ship's *displacement*. Ships that are to sail above water are designed so that they will always weigh less than the water they displace— even when loaded with freight or passengers. Thus they will always be in a state of positive buoyancy —they will float.

Submarines, on the other hand, are designed so that they can change their buoyancy by varying the amount of water they carry in their ballast tanks. If the tanks are empty, the submarine will float on top of the water. If the tanks are filled, the vessel becomes much heavier and sinks, for the water weighs far more than the air which was formerly filling the ballast tanks. Under these conditions, the submarine is said to be in a state of negative buoyancy.

Of course if the tanks are kept full, the submarine will keep on sinking until it reaches the bottom. To prevent plunging too far, the crew must let out some of the water when the vessel reaches the desired depth. But only enough water is let out to keep the submarine at the desired depth. At this stage, the boat is in a state of neither positive nor negative buoyancy. Instead, it is in a condition of *neutral* buoyancy. In other words, it weighs exactly as much as the water it is displacing. It can then be more easily directed up or down while under way.

Only after the Civil War did two American submarine inventors begin to experiment successfully with the principles of neutral and negative buoyancy. And gradually these two men—John Holland and Simon Lake—turned their undersea craft into something besides a deathtrap for heroes.

During the Civil War John Holland had been teaching in a boys' academy in Ireland. On his own he developed an interest in drawing up plans for boats that would travel under water. Newspaper accounts of the Confederate blockade-busting submarines spurred him on to seek new methods.

In 1873 Holland decided to emigrate to America, where he got a job teaching at a parochial school in Paterson, New Jersey. He continued to experiment with designs for submarines, but several years passed before he could secure enough money to start building them in earnest. During a period of twenty-five years, beginning in 1875, Holland launched nine submarines. One of his new ideas was that of using two different motors: an air-breathing gasoline engine for surface running, and a non-breathing electric battery system for traveling under water with a scanty air supply. (A Spaniard by the name of Isaac Peral had already built a submarine which ran by electric motors powered from storage batteries, but the Spanish government refused to recognize the importance of Peral's invention.)

Holland's second boat was able to run under water at a speed of about five or six miles an hour. It contained an air gun for launching a torpedo, but the mechanism never fired accurately.

Holland's boats all operated on the principle of neutral buoyancy. Even when the ballast tanks were completely flooded with water, the boats tended to remain near the surface of the water. Holland depended on his electric motor to push the submarine down. This was accomplished with the aid of diving planes or rudders at the stern. When these were pointed downward, the boat would dive into the water at an angle, very much as a porpoise dives. The idea was to dive below the surface when approaching an enemy ship, pop up again to take a bearing, then quickly dive down to avoid enemy fire and rise again just long enough to release a torpedo.

For many years Holland tried to interest United States Navy officers in the possibilities of his undersea boats. Some of the admirals thought the Irishman was worth watching, but they weren't interested in depriving the surface navy of money to help carry out his radical ideas. Discouraged, Holland was about ready to quit. Suddenly the Navy, changing its mind, announced that it would receive bids for building a submarine. Many inventors in both America and Europe submitted bids, but the contract was finally given to Holland.

The Navy plans called for three propellers, as well as a steam engine to power the ship when it ran on the surface. Holland was sure such a craft would not work, and he was right. The

Plunger, as it was called, proved to be a costly failure.

In the meantime, Holland had been designing a submarine according to his own notions with the backing of private funds. After it was completed, Holland had to promote, demonstrate and test the boat for several years before the Navy would accept it. Finally, on April 18, 1900, the completed submarine was officially purchased—at a loss to Holland. Called the U.S.S. *Holland*, she was the ninth underwater craft built by John Holland, and the first submarine to become a regular part of the United States Navy.

After the stubborn but open-minded Admiral George Dewey watched the *Holland* perform on a trial run, he reported to Congress: "The moral effect—to my mind—is infinitely superior to mines and torpedoes or anything of that kind. . . . With two of those in Galveston, all the navies in the world could not blockade the place."

The *Holland* was just under fifty-four feet long and weighed seventy-four tons. She used a gasoline engine when traveling on the surface and an electric motor when under water. At last the grateful admirals had a long-range submarine that didn't have to be carried into battle like a lifeboat! When under water the *Holland* was supposed to be able to cruise a distance of fifty miles at five knots. On the surface she traveled at eight knots for a much longer distance.

At the bow of the *Holland* there was a tube for shooting torpedoes. The earlier submariners had faced a double risk of death, on account of explosive charges that had to be carried right to the enemy. But in 1868 Robert Whitehead, a Britisher working in Austria, perfected a self-propelled torpedo. This type of weapon had been tried before, but Whitehead designed automatic controls which kept the torpedo on a steady course at a predetermined depth. Armed with the new weapon, Holland's submarine was able to strike from a distance.

By 1903 the United States Navy was enthusiastic enough about the possibilities of the *Holland* to give her inventor a contract for six more similar boats. When finished they formed the world's first fleet of submarines. At first the underwater craft were named after water serpents—*Adder* and *Moccasin*. Then, evidently accepted as fish rather than snakes, the last four were called *Porpoise*, *Shark*, *Grampus* and *Pike*.

The British Admiralty did not make the same

mistake with John Holland that they had made with another Yankee, Robert Fulton. Within a short time they sent a naval officer to Washington with a contract for the American inventor to design submarines for the British navy. Soon the British shipyards were building new Holland undersea craft. The first boats proved to be highly unsuccessful because of British modifications in the designs. But after the first failure the plans were corrected, and workable submarines appeared in the British navy. Many of the young officers were enthusiastic, but the old sea dogs were far from convinced. "Underwater weapons!" snorted the Admiralty's comptroller. "I call them underhand, unfair and . . . un-English. They'll never be any use in war, and I'll tell you why. I'm going to get the First Lord to announce that we intend to treat all submarines as pirate vessels in wartime. We'll hang all their crews."

While Holland was building his first submarines, a boy named Simon Lake was growing up in nearby Pleasantville, New Jersey. At the age of eleven he read *Twenty Thousand Leagues under the*

Sea, Jules Verne's science-fiction fantasy of a trip under the sea. Simon studied the author's description of an underwater vessel as if it were real. And he made notes of improvements he intended to make when he grew up.

But Simon Lake was poor. Not until 1895, when he was twenty-nine, did he finally scrape together enough money to build his first dream, the *Argonaut Junior.* It was a mechanic's submarine, only fourteen feet long. The hull was made up of two layers of plain yellow pine with waterproof canvas between. But the most unusual thing about the craft was that it had three wheels. There were two large ones on either side not far from the bow and a single, smaller wheel back at the stern. The propeller was cranked, Civil War style, because Lake could not afford an engine.

But Simon could do something that had been done by Captain Nemo, hero of *Twenty Thousand Leagues under the Sea.* He could take a walk under water. There was a tiny diving chamber or air lock from which he emerged in a pair of swimming trunks and a diver's helmet to explore the river floor.

The baby *Argonaut Junior* couldn't sink as much

as a rowboat. But it could do something hitherto impossible for submarines. It could make money for its owner without any help from admirals. Lake explored all over the bottoms of harbors. He salvaged anchors from wrecks, pried open the doors of flooded cabins, wrestled with weed-covered ships' safes. With puzzled fish circling around his head, he scraped up enough lost valuables to help pay for building another, larger boat. When one fish watched him for ten hours, Lake said, "He had more interest in our submarine activities than most professors and admirals I knew."

Lake next built *Argonaut I*. She was about thirty-six feet long, with a thirty-horsepower engine. By means of a tricycle undercarriage with seven-foot cast-iron wheels, *Argonaut I* settled on the bottom like a big shrimp. Lake wanted to keep his submarines as simple as possible, so that every family could have one. Instead of all that noisy fuss about filling and emptying tanks to sink and rise, Lake invented a simpler technique for moderate depths. He let go two anchors and dragged them till they caught firmly. Then the anchor chains were wound in and the vessel was hauled to the bottom until she rested on her wheels.

Argonaut I was the first boat in history to be deliberately hauled down below the waves to her anchors instead of having the anchors hauled up to her. But there was a catch: to operate under water she had to release to the surface a breathing tube, so that both her gas engine and her crew could breathe. Lake's tube was an ancestor of the later snorkel or "snout" of the German U-boats.

To prove *Argonaut I* was rugged, Lake took her from Norfolk to New York, submerged under a wild November storm. He snooped at wrecks all the way. "Vessels boarded were coal-lugs, not of much value," the inventor reported modestly. "But the coal would pay handsomely for its recovery." Instead of filling up the cramped *Argonaut* with bags of dripping coal, he rigged a suction pump that lifted the coal to a barge on the surface.

Gradually Lake saw there was money to be made from government submarine contracts, but for a long time he was unable to interest the United States Navy in his undersea boats. Holland had gotten there ahead of him. Nevertheless, Lake built another submarine. This was the 130-ton giant, *Protector*, launched at Bridgeport, Connecticut. The *Protector* worked on a different principle from the Holland submarines. Using both bow and stern planes, it descended on an even keel with slight negative buoyancy instead of plunging headfirst like a porpoise. This technique was later to be copied by the German U-boats.

Simon Lake was also responsible for another advance in submarining. He built a successful periscope from which he could view the surface of the water while the submarine was cruising along submerged. The pilots of Holland's early submarines had been forced to navigate "blind." Lake's periscope was designed to fit a submariner's heart. Not only could it peek above the waves, it could also be turned in any direction. And it could even be hauled down.

By the beginning of the twentieth century, shipyards, admirals and governments all over the world were beginning to cable the two rival American inventors. Lake's advantage was that he was young, while Holland was growing older and less active.

Russia and Japan, arming for war in 1904, sent rival bids to Lake. Many Americans favored the

Japanese, wrongly considering them the under-dogs because they were small. Lake, however, favored the Russians. The Russians had helped an earlier German submarine inventor named William Bauer. And since then their own inventor, Stefan Drzewiecke, had built four Russian sub-marines. Three of them had to be cranked by hand; a fourth ran on batteries.

The government in Washington, sticking to an official policy of neutrality, was worried about Lake's business dealings with the Russian Czar's navy. Lake went ahead anyway. He sold *Protector* to Russia for $250,000. Half of the amount was to be paid at once; the other half was to be paid on delivery. Secretly he hired a coal-carrying freighter and a wrecker's barge with a big crane—ships he knew well from salvaging sunken coal. He ordered this tiny private fleet to wait off Sandy Hook, beyond sight of the Coast Guard.

On a Saturday, the day off for officials, Lake sent *Protector* to sea with a crew of shipyard mechanics. Outside the three-mile limit, in inter-national waters, the submarine met the other two ships. Under cover of a lucky rain squall, the crane lifted up the *Protector* and eased her onto

the deck of the freighter. She was the first submarine in history to be smuggled out of national
boundaries. The *Protector* left the United States,
sitting bone-dry on the blackened decks of a
collier.

Lake spent seven years in Russia, teaching the
businessmen there mass-production methods. He
came back occasionally, his stunt forgiven but
not forgotten. For the Czar's navy he built five
more submarines at Newport News. They were
constructed in two sections, carried off on railroad
flatcars, and then shipped to Russia.

The Japanese, not to be outdone, put five
Holland submarines into service during the Russo-
Japanese conflict. But the submarines never were
used effectively by either side and had little to do
with Japan's eventual victory.

Lake, the one-time poor boy, now wore a
monocle in his left eye. It made him look like a
duke, but that wasn't its purpose. The muscle of
the eye was so strained from peering through the
socket of his periscopes that it wouldn't keep the
eyelid up any more.

Finally the United States Navy expressed an
interest in Lake's submarines. In 1911 he sold

them plans for two colossal submarines: *Seal* and *Tuna*, each 161 feet long. He also let Krupps, the German arms plant, have some of his submarine plans. But when he tried to collect his money, Krupps wouldn't pay. Lake had failed to register his patents in Germany.

Although people thought of submarines mainly as instruments of warfare, Lake never ceased to urge that they be used for peaceful purposes. He dreamed of an underwater freighter cruising under the icy arctic seas, indifferent to the dangerous icebergs of the surface. Throughout the first and second world wars, while U-boats were drowning ships all over the globe, Lake kept insisting that all big ship traffic should go below the storms, under the sea. Huge 7500-ton submarine freighters, as big as cruisers, would be able to avoid bombings and surface sighting. Lake died without knowing that the end of World War II would usher in atomic submarines as big as the giants he had predicted.

5. WORLD WAR I: THE SUBMARINES STRIKE

On August 1, 1914, Germany declared war on Russia. Two days later she made a formal declaration of war against France, at the same time moving troops into neutral Belgium. Immediately Great Britain declared war on Germany. World War I—which would eventually involve many more nations—was under way.

The First World War found two fleets of inexperienced submariners, British and German, skulking along the valleys of the sea, searching for a safe way to kill each other. Neither side really knew how to go about it. The submarine, as a weapon of war, was more than a century old, yet not a single underwater craft had ever sunk a ship and escaped afterward. Submarines had proved dangerous—but mainly to themselves.

The submarine crews, however, were bold and confident. Their new torpedoes could strike from two miles away. Their two-inch-wide periscopes were tall and far-seeing, enabling them to dive when pursuers appeared. Best of all, they had finally received the engine of their dreams: the Diesel.

In 1892 a German engineer named Rudolf Diesel had completed and successfully operated an engine that burned oil. This new engine was cheaper, more efficient and less dangerous to run than the engines that burned gasoline. In the past, poisonous gas fumes in the confined spaces of an underwater submarine hull had been a constant danger to the crew. Small wonder that the men frequently kept a cage of white mice near by. When the mice began to topple over in sleep, the crew knew it was time to bring the boat to the surface for fresh air. The gasoline engines also carried with them the constant threat of a possible fatal explosion. Thus it was a great advance when Diesel found a way to use oil safely. The oil was mixed with air and then compressed so tightly that it exploded by itself, without a spark.

Under the waves the submarine still ran on electric batteries. Although the air was still scarce, it was no longer explosive or poisonous. On the surface, the use of the Diesel engine suddenly gave the submarine long sea legs for the chase. Burning only half as much fuel as the overheated, smelly auto engines, the clean, powerful Diesel took the underwater craft hundreds of miles offshore. From being a timid teaser of blockades, scuttering in and out of ports, the submarine became a bold raider roaming the high seas, able to fight any warship anywhere.

At the outbreak of World War I Germany had twenty-eight *Unterseeboote* (undersea boats). Fourteen were stinking little kerosene burners that gave off telltale plumes of smoke; the rest were racy Diesels, long-finned sharks ready for deep waters. Britain had sixty-four submarines. Forty-seven of them were out of date, underpowered, and prone to explosions. France had more than sixty submarines, many of them very modern for the time. But since German warships seldom put out to sea, there were few targets available for the French underwater vessels.

On September 5, 1914, a rough, white-capped day on the sea, Lieutenant Commander Otto Hersing of the German *U-21* was cruising off St. Abb's Head near the border of England and

Scotland. Suddenly, through his periscope, he saw a long, gray shape slipping through the mist. He brought his prow around, ordering, "All engines full ahead!" Hersing, a tall, dark man, gripped the periscope's handles tightly. When he gave the command, "Steady! Fire!" a torpedo spurted off. Seconds later, just forward of the stranger's funnel, it struck at the water line.

The sea shuddered. The ship, her magazine burst and her bow torn away, nosed over. Her stern climbed helplessly in the air, its white ensign drooping. One lifeboat—the sole hope for 268 terrorized men—dropped away. In only four minutes His Majesty's Ship *Pathfinder*, a small cruiser of 3,200 tons, was a gurgling pool of wreckage, gone forever. Five men were killed by the explosion and sixteen wounded, but two hundred and fifty-five went down, mostly trapped below decks.

Pathfinder was the first ship ever to be successfully sunk by a fully submerged submarine. But Hersing did not know he had started his record with a cruiser until spies in Holland sent in the report. He was soon to become one of the most famous submariners of the war.

This first stroke of thunder was only the warn-

ing note of what was to come next from the
undreamed-of power of the U-boats. On September
22, three torpedo blows struck home in less than
two hours. They ended forever a ten-thousand-year
domination of the sea by ships that sailed on the
surface.

Blond, quiet Lieutenant Otto Weddigen was
patrolling in the *U-9*, a smoky, out-of-date kerosene
burner, along the shallow waters of Holland.
Suddenly he saw three gray warships, each with
four stacks, steaming toward him. "Attack stations!" he ordered. But the Lieutenant was afraid
his little craft might leap from the water like a
dolphin when its three heavy torpedoes were
launched. So he added, "After firing, dive to
fifteen meters [forty-nine feet]."

At 500 yards he shot his first torpedo, dived,
heard a crash, came up and found a cruiser
sinking in a cloud of steam. Her stern was already wet. Weddigen dived again, loaded both
his bow tubes, came up and peeked. Another
cruiser was picking up survivors. A second torpedo
hissed its farewell, and *U-9* dived again. By this
time the little kerosene burner was so unstable
under water that the Lieutenant could get her

nose up or down only by bunching his crew amidships and chasing them like chickens, forward or astern.

Driving his crew aft, Weddigen rose and peeked again. This time he saw two cruisers sinking and a third standing loyally by, picking up swimmers. He turned *U-9* about, so he could get away quickly, and fired both his stern torpedoes. One of them made a hit, but the damage did not appear to be great. Had he been observed? Apparently not. In the foaming water and swirling wreckage, it was difficult to see what was happening.

His last torpedo was in the bow tube. He turned *U-9* again, bow on. "Fire! Periscope in! All hands forward! Dive!" They were barely under when a crash rang out as the torpedo's nose struck. Then came the roar of internal explosion. He turned away and, coming up, saw a terrible panorama. The third cruiser, hit more vitally than the other two, was turning on her side, spilling the would-be rescuers from her deck.

Not until *U-9* arrived home at Kiel did Weddigen learn that he had sunk three heavily armed 12,000 tonners: *Aboukir, Hogue* and *Cressy*. Thirty-six thousand tons had been murdered in an hour at the cost of only five torpedoes. Just 777 men were saved out of 2,100 sailors, and half the 120 officers went to the bottom. Weddigen, to show he was more than lucky, went out again, tracked the cruiser *Hawke* and sank her. This time there was only one boatful of survivors. His little boat became the "lucky *U-9*."

But warships were not the only vessels sunk. On October 20, another German submarine, the small *U-17*, though under strict orders to sink only warships, stopped and searched the British freighter *Glitra*. The Germans found nothing but sewing machines and whiskey in the merchant ship, but they ordered the British mariners to their lifeboats and opened the sea cocks. In a few minutes the *Glitra's* stack slipped under the water line, and she was only a chain of bubbles. History had been made again. Though not torpedoed, *Glitra* became the first of some 50,000 useful freighters, liners, tankers, trawlers, yachts, light-ships, colliers, schooners, tugs and barges drowned by man's wasteful hand. The *Glitra's* crew members, however, were luckier than thousands who followed them. They lived.

John P. Holland, designer and builder of the USS *Holland* (below), the U. S. Navy's first submarine.

Above: Simon Lake's submarine *Argonaut* in the Chesapeake, off Baltimore.

Opposite: Three World War I submarines. *Top to bottom:* the American *L-3*, the British *E-7* and the German *U-9*. The latter sank three British warships in less than two hours, thereby challenging Britain's control of the seas.

German submarine aces of World War I. *Above:* Otto Hersing, indicated by an "X," carried out the first successful sinking of a warship by a fully submerged submarine. *Below:* The sporting Lothar von Arnauld (second from left) always gave his victims advance warning before attacking.

Veterans of two World Wars. *Above:* German Admiral Karl
Doenitz. *Below:* British Admiral Sir Max Horton (right).

An American destroyer protects the flank of a convoy against submarine attack.

thank you!

Above: A depth charge is exploded during a phase of naval training.

Top left: Crew members load an electric torpedo aboard a U. S. submarine at an advanced base.

Bottom left: A burning Allied tanker sinks after being torpedoed by a U-boat.

Planes from a U. S. carrier drop bombs on an enemy U-boat.

Commander Donald Mac-
intyre, the British officer
whose destroyers sank
U-boat aces Prien and
Schepke.

Guenther Prien, the U-boat captain who attacked the home port of the British Grand Fleet.

A British underwater "Chariot" or human torpedo, with its driver at the controls.

Opposite: The gentleman with the black tie is Lt. Comdr. Richard H. O'Kane, whose submarine *Tang* surfaced and whisked 22 carrier-based pilots out of the waters near Truk—one of the most daring rescues of the Pacific War.

A Japanese midget submarine beached off Bellows Field, Hawaii.

U-boat *505* was captured intact thanks to the bold resourcefulness and courage of Captain Daniel V. Gallery and the crew of the USS *Guadalcanal*.

Left: The salvage crew is at work aboard the captured sub. *Right:* Captain Gallery poses in the U-boat commander's confiscated cap.

Lt. Comdr. Howard W. Gilmore (left) of USS *Growler* and
Comdr. Samuel Dealey (right) of USS *Harder*.

The USS *Sculpin*, finally sunk by the Japanese in November of 1943, was one
of the first American submarines to see active duty in the Pacific Theater.

A common hunting ground for both British and German submarines was the North Sea fishing banks. Here weak little wooden trawlers, both British and German, netted the herring side by side. All at once these unfortunate fishermen found themselves caught in the middle of a submarine war. Few torpedoes were used. The submariners on both sides, perhaps a little ashamed to be chasing trawlers, tried to be as decent as they could.

A submarine would surface a few yards from a trawler full of fishermen dressed in rough sweaters and scaly oilskins and armed only with fish knives. An officer would appear on the sub's deck with a megaphone. "Get off! You'll be sunk in five minutes!" he would warn. Then, after the crew had rowed away, the submariners would sink the little boat by using their deck gun.

Such hunting looked as safe as duck shooting, but it could be dangerous. The German *U-81* saw a freighter and surfaced, warning the ship's crew to lower their boats. Then the U-boat began pounding the freighter's water line with shells. But unknown to either attacker or victim the British submarine *E-54* was watching. While *U-81* was enjoying her shooting, with her back turned, two British torpedoes struck. As the *U-81* slid down into the sea, the *E-54* began picking up seven of her gun crew from her deck, including the captain. When he was dragged aboard, choking from sea water, the German gurgled: "Look out, captain! You may be sunk, too! We have another U-boat near by."

The *E-54* escaped.

In time the British figured out a way to trick the German submarines by using a fishing trawler as bait. The stained, smoky trawler would slowly plow along with her nets dragging in the water. Unseen, a British submarine followed in the fisherman's boiling wake, submerged only a few feet. The staccato mutter of the trawler's engine concealed the thrash of the sub's propellers. From the trawler's bridge a telephone cable, concealed in the nets, trailed back to the creeping submarine.

The submarine commander waited patiently until he received the eagerly awaited warning: "U-boat sighted!" As soon as he heard gunfire, he used his periscope to get a bearing on the enemy submarine. Then he closed in and fired his torpedoes. Frequently he made a killing.

The Germans matched this trick by disguising a U-boat as a trawler. The Germans painted deceptive lines to simulate a trawler's bow and stern. They mounted fake masts and a funnel that could be stepped down horizontally when the U-boat submerged. Fishing nets hung from the false rigging. At a distance, the U-boat looked like a water-swamped trawler drying out its nets.

Next the British started secretly building "Q" or mystery ships. These were fast, heavily gunned merchantmen disguised as slow, timid freighters. When a U-boat broke water and fired its warning shot, the Q-ship's radio would flash an uncoded signal, "Am attacked by U-boat." Then a well-rehearsed "panic party" of sailors would rush for the boats. The radio would flash, "Am abandoning ship" and give the position.

Reassured by overhearing the frightened radio messages, the U-boat would creep closer. The "panic party" would continue its performance, upsetting lifeboats and delaying departure. Meantime, through the upper portholes, expert gunners were taking aim at the submarine. Suddenly the iron bulkheads fell with a crash, the white navy ensign ran up the mast, and scores of shells perforated the U-boat.

Q-ships sank thirteen U-boats before the Germans fully caught on. One crafty British naval officer, Captain Gordon Campbell, became famous for his success in sinking enemy submarines by the use of this trick.

Meanwhile, British submarine commanders were beginning to win their share of glory. Max Horton, a lieutenant destined to be a master submariner in two world wars, commanded the 800-ton *E-9*, armed with only five torpedo tubes. Itching to revenge Weddigen's sinking of Britain's three cruisers, he was lying at dawn in the bay between Germany's naval base on the island of Helgoland and the German mainland. A gray shape came purring out of the fog. Into its armor plate he fired two torpedoes. He dived, joyfully heard two crashes, came up, and "walked the periscope" around the horizon. The water was filled with swimming Germans. He had hit the cruiser *Hela*, the first capital ship sunk by a British submarine.

Destroyers raced vengefully out of Helgoland, peppering the water with underwater charges. Horton crept away on his batteries, but they grew weak. He came up for a glance, right into a nightmare. He was speeding along in formation with a German destroyer. Turning a little he fired on the dead run and got "maximum luck." As he later wrote in his log: "She went up beautifully and after five minutes all that was to be seen was about fifteen feet of bow sticking up vertically out of the water."

The British admirals began proudly calling Horton "our pirate." Horton accepted the title, made himself a skull and crossbones, and flew it from his conning tower. Other young commanders rallied around him.

Another British submarine lieutenant, Norman Holbrook, carried out a dangerous mission in the clear shallow waters of the Mediterranean Sea. Here the British and French were trying to break through the defenses of Turkey, which had come into the war on the German side. The test came in the Dardanelles. Between the narrow brown cliffs where the Black Sea joins the Aegean, two fleets and two armies—British and French—were trying vainly to break through the Turkish mine fields, searchlights and coastal guns. Their ultimate objective was to get supplies into Russia.

A ten-year-old scrap-heap submarine, the 143-

foot *B-11*, was outfitted with fenders to sweep aside mines. With a crew of eleven men, the daring Lieutenant Holbrook took his little underwater craft through five rows of mines, came up to the surface, and found a two-stack Turkish battleship, the *Messoudieh*, near by. He ran up to within a half mile of her and fired one torpedo. She rolled over and sank in ten minutes.

On the way out again *B-11's* compass failed, and the fast current swept her onto a sand bank. Yet she managed to pull loose and escape. Holbrook was awarded the Victoria Cross for his feat.

But it was the German U-boats, coming from 3,000 miles away, that settled the Dardanelles conflict. The British and French warships had set up a blockade. Defending the trenches of Gallipoli, their big guns pounded the Turkish shore batteries unmercifully. Then came an unpleasant surprise. The 12,000-ton battleship *Triumph* was holding her place in the blockade when suddenly a torpedo "went through her torpedo net like a clown jumping through a paper hoop." She turned over and sank in hissing steam, taking with her seventy-one stokers trapped in her engine room. Who did it?

It was *U-21*. The U-boat had been brought through the Mediterranean by her commander, Otto Hersing, to crack the blockade from outside.

Next Hersing slipped within 600 yards of the old battleship *Majestic*, fired a single perfect torpedo, and saw her go down, carrying forty-eight trapped firemen in her hull. The impudent Hersing then crept through both the British and French mine fields and anchored by the mosques of Constantinople. Under the protection of his Turkish allies, he repainted his number, changing it to *U-51* to pretend that two U-boats were operating in the area. After filling his tanks with Turkish oil, he stole out again. The fleets withdrew; the blockade ended. Britain put a half-million-dollar reward on his head, but nobody collected. Five years after the war France was still offering $25,000 for him.

6. THE U-BOATS AT BAY

From the outset of World War I, the United States insisted on freedom of the seas to supply Britain through the U-boat blockade. At first the German U-boats respected her neutrality. Then the German High Command realized that their own fleet could have little effect on British sea power. Supplies kept flowing into Britain from America. On the other hand, the British naval blockade of Germany was slowly strangling the German nation. Vital food supplies and other required materials were no longer getting in. German U-boat commanders were ordered to cease to observe the established rules of surface warfare.

In May of 1915 the *Lusitania*, a huge British liner carrying guns and ammunition, as well as passengers, sailed from New York for Liverpool. The Germans had warned that she would be sunk, and they kept their word. The liner remained afloat only twenty minutes after Commander Walther von Schweiger of the *U-20* fired a single, old-fashioned bronze-headed torpedo into her boiler room. Here is what von Schweiger saw through his periscope:

"There was a terrible panic on deck. Overcrowded lifeboats, fairly torn from their positions, dropped into the water. Desperate women ran helplessly up and down the decks. Men and women jumped into the water and tried to swim to empty, overturned lifeboats. It was the most terrible sight I have ever seen. Impossible for me to give any help. I could have saved only a handful." The *Lusitania* went down, taking with her 1,198 passengers, including 128 Americans.

What was a U-boat skipper's duty? To warn beforehand every vessel he sank, whether Q-ship or tramp, gun-runner or trawler? Some submarine captains said: "It's their life or ours. No warning."

But the most deadly submariner of all took pride in always giving warning. He was the incredible Lothar von Arnauld de la Perière of *U-35* and *U-139*. Starting six months after the *Lusitania* sank, he personally brought down more

than 195 ships, a half million tons. No other captain in any war ever matched his record. In a
single twenty-four-day patrol, with his little forty-
man boat, he sank fifty-four ships. A British submarine almost torpedoed *U-35* twice, first with a
torpedo that leaped like a flying fish and landed
humming on the sub's deck, and then with another
that ran dangerously deep. But the chivalrous
Arnauld continued warning ships, sinking them,
and escaping.

From Washington, D. C., the German ambas-
sador warned his government in Berlin that the
United States might enter the war if the U-boats
did not ease up. Whereupon the Germans offered to trade peacefully with the United States
as a neutral, using submarines as cargo carriers.
Dodging under the British fleet, the huge U-boat
Deutschland twice carried German dyes to Baltimore
and New London.

With her ever growing U-boat fleet now up to
a total of 148, Germany seemed close to victory.
In January of 1917, she changed her policy again
and ordered "unrestricted submarine warfare,"
extending the war zone to cover the high seas.
By that time 2,431 ships had been sunk—9 out

of 10 by U-boats. American anger flared up at the word "unrestricted." The U-boats were sinking one out of every four ships leaving a British port. In a single day they sent down eleven merchantmen and gunned eight trawlers to death.

On April 6, 1917, the United States formally declared war. In June American forces began landing in France. And the United States Navy began sending destroyers, all armed with depth charges, to spoil the happy hunting of the U-boats. Freighters carried to Europe thousands of mines to make miserable the outward voyage and homecoming of the U-boats through the North Sea. The 230-mile "Northern Barrage" from Scotland to Norway was a belt 15 to 35 miles wide (with a 1-mile-wide secret channel) hung with 70,263 of these horned basketballs of death. More than 56,000 of them had been shipped from the United states.

One night eighteen U-boats, armed with flares, tried to swarm through the triple barrier of mines, searchlights and picketboats. Only two survived this rash undersea charge.

The first American warship to be torpedoed by an enemy submarine was the *Jacob Jones*, a

destroyer. Hans Rose, captain of the U-boat, surfaced and helped the swimming crewmen to
reach their life rafts. He even flashed a radio
rescue call for them.

After America's entry into the war, a group of
German submarines started raiding off America's
Atlantic coast. One of them, the *U-151* under
Commander von Nostitz, spread scores of mines
in Delaware Bay and sank 23 ships with gunfire
and torpedoes in the 94 days of a 10,915-mile
voyage. The *U-151* was one of a new giant class
of U-boats the Germans were just beginning to
build—a forerunner of the submarine of the
future. Had these new giants been ready for
operation earlier, the course of the war at sea
might have been changed.

The Americans, aware that they were far behind in submarine development, yearned to capture a U-boat to study. They almost got *U-58*.
Two "ashcans"—depth charges dropped by a
destroyer—drove her downward with her diving
fins jammed. At 278 feet, on the point of being
crushed by the depths, Captain Amberger desper-
ately blew the water out of all his tanks. Up
came the *U-58* like a cork. She popped out of

water under the prow of a United States destroyer. Her deck crew scrambled out, ready to surrender. But they had already opened her sea cocks, and the water was gushing in. The *U-58* took half her crew and all her secrets to the bottom with her.

As the German army was pushed back on the continent, the U-boats lost their advanced bases on the French coast. Once the Americans got into the war, 16,539 ships defied the U-boats and only 102 of these were sunk. Of the two million American troops who sailed for France, only 126 were lost to U-boats. The German public, accustomed to victory, demanded an explanation. One of their admirals reported: "The Americans have dozens of landing places. Their convoys have not been arriving with the regularity and frequency of railroad trains in a station, but irregularly, at great intervals of time and often in night or fog." The convoys were also well protected.

When Germany collapsed it was her proud U-boat crews, still unbeaten in their own eyes, who tried to put down the mutinies among the crews on the Imperial Navy's surface warships. Though the undersea fleet had lost 199 submarines, they still had 138 left. And they had sunk 18,716,782 tons—more than 5,000 ships, about half of them British.

At the end of the war the United States Navy asked President Woodrow Wilson to obtain a few captured U-boats for them to study. At first Wilson, wanting no rewards of victory for America, refused. Finally he agreed to ask for six submarines as exhibits for a Victory Loan drive. But the American request came too late. The cupboard of the German naval bases was bare. The proud U-boat men had sunk the best of their fleet, secrets and all. The British, French and Japanese navies had seized most of the workable U-boats that remained.

Of 164 surrendered U-boats lying at Harwich, England, the Americans got six, including one minelayer. The best, *U-111*, was able to cross to New York without refueling. The others took twenty-four days to cross by way of the Azores. Even the Middle West got a look at a U-boat. The minelayer *UC-97*, under command of Lieutenant Charles A. Lockwood, Jr., threaded through the St. Lawrence River and the Great Lakes, and was received with wonder in Quebec, Montreal and Chicago.

The Americans copied the German Diesels. The *U-111* was even attached for a year to the Atlantic fleet. She had three periscopes with fine Austrian lenses. Her decks were nonskid teak, ideal for loading. Her "wet" guns could be fired immediately on surfacing, without dangerous delays. "The bridge, hull, periscope, guns, torpedo tubes, machinery and compartment design of the *U-111* were far superior to our submarines," reported one American naval officer. Her organs were removed for duplication, including her engines, motor generators, air compressors, tank blowers and gyroscope.

Too late the United States had learned how dangerous it could be to fall behind in submarine warfare.

7. U-BOATS
AGAIN

Americans called World War I "the war to end wars," but they were wrong. Germany was humiliated by her defeat and angered by what she considered unfair peace terms. She wanted revenge. And in 1933 she got a leader—Adolf Hitler—who was determined to achieve this aim. From the beginning Hitler made no secret of the fact that he planned to take over the rule of all Europe—and eventually the world. But it was some time before other countries began to take him seriously.

Under the terms of a naval agreement Hitler negotiated with England in 1935, Germany's navy was to be limited to 35% of the naval strength maintained by Great Britain. But she was allowed to have 45% as many submarines as England. And under certain circumstances she could increase her allotment to 100%. This was an unbelievable agreement in view of the damage inflicted by German submarines during the First World War.

On September 1, 1939, a German army invaded Poland. There could no longer be any doubt about Hitler's ambitions. Quickly his well-trained troops overran Norway and Denmark, Holland, Belgium and France. Finally only Great Britain was left to withstand the savage onslaught of Hitler's fighting force. (Both Italy and Russia were siding with Germany at the outset of the war.)

In spite of the terms of her agreement with Great Britain, Germany actually had fifty-six submarines when the war began. England herself had just fifty-seven. The Germans had also been building heavier warships than their public announcements indicated.

The new U-boat commander, Admiral Karl Doenitz, expected his underwater fleet to be bottled up by deadly mine fields as in World War I. So as quickly as possible he sent all his seagoing submarines out to sea beyond the British nets. (Only eight of the U-boats could operate in mid-Atlantic, and only thirteen carried enough fuel to be able to circle the British Isles.)

The British laid five walls of mines across the

English Channel, destroying three U-boats that tried to take short cuts. The U-boats were forced to circle completely around Scotland and Ireland to blockade the southern English ports, thereby wasting several days' food and fuel.

In World War I, ninety-seven per cent of the U-boat attacks had been by daylight, the rest by full moon. But in World War II the submarines struck on dark nights, too. At high tide on a moonless night in October, 1939, Lieutenant Guenther Prien guided *U-47* into Scapa Flow. This corkscrew bay amidst the Orkney Islands off the north coast of Scotland served as home port for the British Grand Fleet. Prien stole along the surface, under the long white fingers of searchlights. He dared not dive. His running speed submerged was only five knots, slower than the current of the running tide, which would be able to pull and haul him at its mercy.

Prien threaded around submerged block ships, huge rocks, and through a cable net. (Most of the fleet had been ordered out a couple of days earlier.) Aiming by the wild glitter of the northern lights, he fired three torpedoes at the old battleship *Royal Oak*. Only one of them hit, glancingly. The jolt was so slight to her thick armor that her officers thought some heavy tool had fallen below decks. No alarm was sounded.

Prien backed away, astonished. Were the British this tough? Well, he would try again. Within twenty minutes he reloaded his tubes, then fired. This time two torpedoes struck through the steel hide. Almost at once the battleship turned over, taking 24 officers and 809 sailors, mostly sleeping in their hammocks, down into the icy dark. Prien escaped, fighting the current every inch of the way.

Unable to keep up a constant patrol of British ports, the U-boats sowed magnetic mines wherever they could, especially at the mouth of the Thames. In return, the British darkened their lightships and made the swept channels hard to find.

At first the handful of German U-boats stayed away from guarded convoys. They attacked only ships that were too slow or fast for protected escort. Yet in four months they sank nearly 200 ships, 114 by torpedoes and 79 by mines. But Britain still ate well, thanks to the huge, guarded convoys.

Then Hitler's troops seized Atlantic harbors in

France and Norway. The short range of the U-boats was suddenly lengthened. Their torpedo attacks drew 450 miles nearer to America. No more wasteful journeys around Scotland! Even little 250-ton U-boats carrying only a week's fuel were darting deep into the open Atlantic.

By October of 1940 the German shipyards were pouring out new hulls and the underwater fleet was growing. The young U-boat commanders— their average age was in the mid-twenties—began to enjoy what they called "our happy time." The British aircraft carriers were hiding and destroyers were scarce. Freighters bound empty for Canada scattered like seagulls in mid-Atlantic, giving up their destroyer escort to the deep-laden convoys of freighters bound for Europe. The U-boats gaily knocked off these unprotected slowpokes. Other U-boats waited for incoming convoys off the north-west coast of Ireland.

Growing bolder, the German submariners began attacking on the surface of the north Atlantic all through the long nights. In a scant four months they sank 144 unescorted ships. They even bored into convoys, sinking 73 freighters under the noses of the worried destroyers. With their newly acquired advanced air bases, they were able to search for convoys with four-motored Kondor patrol planes. On the dreadful "night of the long knives"—October 18, 1940—three U-boat aces, Prien, Joachim Schepke and Otto Kretschmer, led a pack of 12 U-boats. They sank 31 ships in two convoys totaling 83 ships. Between dusk and dawn 150,000 tons went down.

As U-boats multiplied, Admiral Doenitz dropped lone attacks. Instead he started "wolf packs," bands of from ten to twenty submarines. First a roving Kondor patrol plane flashed the word "convoy sighted" to U-boat headquarters at Lorient on the French coast. Then Doenitz sent an attacking plan to the commanding submarine of the nearest wolf pack. Only one or two U-boats attacked at first, trying to pull away the destroyers and the little bulldog corvettes. Then suddenly twenty submarines popped up on the edges of the convoy, firing torpedoes at close range.

The young U-boat captains even dared to surface before attacking convoys by night. At first the only device tracking them was "asdic," a kind of submarine feeler developed after World

War I. Americans called it "sonar." It listened to U-boats under water.

A destroyer sending out the pinging asdic signals under water could bounce them off a submarine, provided she was submerged and not over a mile away. But the submarine had to be straight ahead to be heard clearly. If she was astern, or trailing on either flank, asdic was almost deaf, because of the bubbling turmoil of the wake. And if the submarine dived, asdic could not tell how deep she went. Asdic was about as useful as the extended hands of a blind man walking among trees. It could, however, listen to propeller turns and tell the difference between a submarine and another ship.

Asdic bothered the wolf packs little. By daylight the young U-boat aces used their periscopes and aimed torpedoes from a safe distance of three or more miles. By night they ran surfaced beside convoys, using their binoculars for spotting. Kretschmer caught two merchant cruisers, *Laurentic* and *Patroclus*, returning from hunting U-boats. She sank both on the same day. Kretschmer's motto was "one ship, one torpedo." He even broke Doenitz' orders by surfacing inside convoys and shooting in all directions instead of merely one.

The wolf packs were weakest when they were out in the "Black Pit" of the mid-Atlantic, beyond range of the sharp-eyed Kondors. Here, without planes to patrol overhead, the U-boats had to scout for themselves, finding convoys and flashing their position to Doenitz. In the convoy, when radio operators heard the sputter of the U-boat's aerial, they knew trouble was near. The wet antennas made a special noise. The convoy could even tell where the attack was coming from with the help of a device called "huff-duff," short for high-frequency direction finder. This gadget could tell where the signaling member of the wolf pack was located.

Soon two other new devices began to interfere with the U-boats. Both were aimed at breaking up night attacks by surfaced U-boats. One was "snow," the other "radar."

Snow was a shower of fireworks fired into the air over the convoy. It illuminated the long black hulls of the U-boats. Of course snow could be used only after the U-boat's first torpedo had struck. And the burning rain lighted up the fleeing ships as well as the submarines.

Radar was an electric eye that raked the sea's surface in all directions, seeing through the

darkest night unless curtained off by rain. An
outline of the unseen ship appeared on a screen,
outlined magically by tiny pips of light. Both
sides had radar, but the Allies, putting theirs on
masts higher than the low-slung U-boats, could
see much farther.

This early radar could pick up a U-boat
twenty miles away, provided the waves were not
running so high that they concealed her low
profile. But the Germans quickly came up with a
special infrared paint intended to throw off the
radar's tracking finger. Sometimes U-boats tried
to jam radar with opposing waves. They sent up
a device called "Aphrodite." This was a bulgy
silver balloon tied to a wooden float and hung
with long aluminum streamers to give the Allied
radar a falsely high image, like a full-sized ship.

After two years of war 100 German U-boats
were on the prowl and another 230 were being
assembled. Then the United States lent 50 elderly
destroyers to Britain. Now convoys could be
escorted all the way across the Atlantic, instead of
only halfway. The Germans answered by building
faster. But in the bitter mid-Atlantic, the U-boats
began wasting many days and missing targets, for
the convoys were becoming more and more alert.

The methodical Doenitz had always insisted on keeping half his U-boat crews in training, at home. Now he ordered the wolf packs to pull back closer to Europe's shores. He wanted them to attack closer, shoot oftener and get back home for a rest sooner.

The German admiral next gave an order which American submarines were to copy later against the Japanese. To get rid of the pesky American destroyers lent to Britain, Doenitz ordered the U-boats to ease up on freighters and aim first at destroyers and escorts. So far only these warships had the deadly radar. By sinking them, the U-boats could blind the convoy.

In the early months of 1941, Doenitz began losing his beloved aces. Caught on the surface at night by the sweeping eye of radar, they dived for safety as they had formerly done. But times had changed. The fumbling fingers of the half-blind asdic, having been shown the U-boat's direction by radar, could now point straight at her and follow her dive down. Depth charges could be dropped more accurately and much sooner.

March, 1941, was a sad month for the Nazi

underwater fighters. Within a single week Prien, Schepke and Kretschmer—three top aces—were put out of action by depth charges from destroyers. Prien and Schepke were both killed; Kretschmer was taken prisoner. Admiral Doenitz had to think up new devices to keep the new commanders unworried by the loss of their idolized pioneers. To enable the submarine crews to strike from farther away, he gave them a torpedo with a magnetic exploder. This exploder was supposed to be activated by the magnetism of the target. When it blew up, it would break the ship's back and sink her. The exploder proved to be unreliable, however, and British engineers soon learned how to demagnetize their ships.

Then new U-boats were fitted with special chambers of oil, garbage and fake wreckage. During a severe depth charge, the U-boat hid as deep as 500 feet, then emptied these wastebaskets upward. While the destroyers were gloating over the wreckage, the U-boat was softly stealing away at one or two knots.

Doenitz' best trick was the *pillenwerfer* or pill thrower. The Allies called it the *SBT*, an abbreviation for "submarine bubble target." The U-boat carried attached outside its hull a small boxful of chemicals. When released, the chemicals produced an intense layer of gas bubbles which gave an echo on the asdic or sonar machine similar to that of a submarine. While the destroyers mistakenly dropped depth charges on the bubbles, the U-boat sank to safer depths and quietly crept away.

Under water the sharp pinging of the asdic was still the U-boat's most feared enemy. When the pinging came faster, the crunching depth charges soon followed. And there was one sound the cleverest engineers of Doenitz could never fake. It was the slow popping of pressure hulls, like crushed peanut shells, as a wounded U-boat sank into the endless depths.

After going beyond a depth of five or six hundred feet, the skinny armor of the U-boat hulls broke. This flooded the submarine. Down, down, down, she sank, hugged ever tighter by the sea. Then, faint from the depths, came the final yielding grunt, the sound of the steel-like cage of the hull folding inward.

Members of the wolf pack heard these sounds even when their own boat escaped. Silently they asked themselves: "Who is down this time? Which berth at Lorient will be empty when we go home?" From under water the crackup sounded, as they expressed it, "like the crushing of an egg crate." This last helpless grunt from a smothered submarine manned by their comrades haunted their dreams and embittered even a safe home-coming. "Who's next? Me?"

8. BRITISH SUBMARINES AND ITALIAN MIDGETS

Starting with John Holland's early "A" boats, the British established a tradition of naming their submarines by letters. For forty years they changed the letters with each new design and the numbers with each different boat. Finally they reached the letters T, U and V. At that point the rebellious British submariners refused to say, "I'm in a U-boat." Instead they decided to baptize their submarines themselves, taking names invented under water, like *Uproar*, *Seadog* and *Trespasser*. They even stole names from destroyers. Soon these nicknames began to be accepted. The officers gradually yielded and gave submarines regular launchings with names of fish, such as *Surf*, *Porpoise* and *Tarpon*, and more unusual ones like *Statesman*, *Subtle*, *Sleuth* and *Thorn*.

Winston Churchill, Britain's Prime Minister, encouraged the rebels. Every submarine deserved

some name, he insisted, even freakish names like
Unbending and *Upright*. As commander of the
World War II underwater fleet, Churchill chose
Vice-Admiral Max Horton, "the pirate" of World
War I. Horton started the war with fifty-seven
submarines, one more than his enemy Doenitz.
But while the U-boats had thousands of freighters
as targets, the British had almost nothing easy,
safe and numerous to shoot at. Germany's food
arrived by railroad, not by sea.

So Horton decided to hunt the hunters, the
U-boats. "Sink at sight, anywhere" were his
orders. To ambush U-boats the British submarines
lay in the narrow exit corridors that led to the
Atlantic. They hid in the mine-strewn Baltic Sea
and the icy fiords of Norway. These shallow
coastal waters, where Horton had gaily scouted as
a World War I lieutenant, were now far more
dangerous. Fast enemy dive bombers cruised
overhead, able to pounce in seconds.

Horton's sub hunters were the first international
submarine fleet in the world. He had refugee
sharks from Holland, Norway, Poland and France,
each with its odd torpedo sizes and gadgets.
Though there were no food ships for the pirates

to sink, they boldly captured Norwegian freighters carrying iron ore for Germany. And they hunted U-boats as far north as Iceland and the North Cape.

By one freak capture of a U-boat, the British got a peek at some of Germany's newest devices. The *U-570*, on her maiden voyage, was surprised off Iceland by a bomber. The novice crew spun their diving controls too late. The bomber, with four carefully planted depth charges, flushed the leaking submarine to the surface. Seamen waving white towels scurried out of the smashed conning tower. The bomber did circles overhead, calling for a destroyer. The *U-570* was taken over by the British, renamed the *Graph*, and sent out again as bait for other U-boats.

British submarines had more opportunity to go after German and Italian shipping in the sunny and translucent—hence dangerous—waters of the Mediterranean. Their bases were at Alexandria in Egypt, and at Malta, a rocky island between Sicily and Africa.

The submarines saved Malta, which suffered under daily bombing raids. While German and Italian bombs were raining on the island, the submarines crouched like green lobsters on the harbor bottom, snug among the seaweeds. But when the bombers were away, the submarines came up and unloaded stores of supplies for the desperate little island. They brought in 167,000 gallons of fuel in a single month, plus 30 tons of food and medicine, 6 tons of shells for the anti-aircraft guns, 12 tons of mail and 124 passengers.

The British underwater men knew every corner and hideout of the Aegean and Adriatic seas and their islands. And they excelled at smuggling in agents. A submarine slipped the American general Mark Clark into Algiers before the city surrendered, and took out the pro-Allied French General Giraud.

Having no massed convoys to shoot at, the British perfected a technique for ambushing big liners racing at high speed. They laid traps in the narrow Mediterranean passages. Lieutenant Commander David Wanklyn in *Upholder*, lying surfaced at three in the morning, received a warning from another submarine that three huge liners were speeding toward him. The giants turned out to be the 24,500-ton *Vulcania* and the twin 19,500-tonners *Neptunia* and *Oceania*. Wanklyn fired a spread of four torpedoes, neatly fanned out. He hit the twin liners, sinking one, wounding the other. Italian destroyers angrily drove him down. But he daringly came up again, with the blinding morning sun behind him and got off two more torpedoes, sinking the wounded liner.

The submarines were worth as much to Britain as a second army in Africa. The Germans admitted that 45% of their losses were due to submarines. In a three-year period the British sank 1,300,000 tons, a tremendous score considering that the convoys bound from Italy to Africa were exposed for only one or two nights.

The British lost forty-one of their submarines in the clear, shallow Mediterranean Sea. But they evened their losses by sinking exactly seventy-four Italian submersibles and U-boats.

In the tricky narrow and congested Mediterranean, submarines depended on spies ashore to warn them of the presence of enemy targets. Because of the many harbors, the best submarine was a small one, able to creep under nets. The Italians found the answer in a pocket submarine as handy as a scooter: the "human torpedo."

The submariner became a jockey, riding his

own torpedo. Carrying terrible explosive power in his hands, he was able to sneak right up to within arm's length of his enemy. The Italians rode in teams of two. With rubber masks and oxygen lungs that gave no bubbles, they could plunge to a depth of eighty feet and endure water as cold as fifty degrees. To get in the vicinity of the target, they rode a big, comfortable mother submarine. After transferring to their sea horses and reaching their destination, they were supposed to suspend the warhead under their target and make their way back to the parent sub or crawl ashore and hide, awaiting pickup.

On the night of December 20, 1941, six Italians rode three midgets, nicknamed "pigs," into the harbor of Alexandria in Egypt. Led by Lieutenant Commander de la Penne, they sneaked through the British anti-submarine nets and managed to attach their explosive warheads to two warships— the *Valiant* and the *Queen Elizabeth*—and a merchantman. Setting delayed action fuses, they sank their pigs and swam quickly away.

De la Penne and one of his crewmen were caught clinging to a huge steel buoy. They were taken aboard the nearby *Valiant* and questioned.

De la Penne told the British captain that the ship would shortly blow up, but he refused to say where he had placed the torpedo. The captain sent him to a cell below the water line to sweat out the coming explosion. Though de la Penne didn't know it at the time, his cell door was unlocked.

B-A-N-G! came the explosion. The *Valiant* settled with a huge hole, but the shallow harbor bottom held her up. De la Penne, discovering that his door was open, rushed on deck in time to see the *Queen Elizabeth's* hull and double bottom burst open. Next the merchantman exploded. All six of the Italians were captured and held as prisoners of war. But they had every reason to be proud, for they had put two British battleships and a merchantman out of commission for a long time to come. The cunning Italian sea horses eventually sank or damaged fourteen ships. And they posed such a threat they were able to tie up several British warships.

Quickly catching on, the British proceeded to develop midget submarines approximately fifty feet long and six feet in diameter. They were usually manned by crews of four, and they carried two huge crescent-shaped packages of amatol weighing two tons each. These "eggs" were to be sunk delicately on the harbor bottom under anchored warships, thus avoiding any noisy tapping on the hull. The British also built even smaller underwater craft which resembled the Italian sea horses. They called them "chariots."

All during the early years of World War II, the Royal Navy dreamed of sinking the mighty German battleship *Tirpitz*. Most of the time she remained hidden in Norwegian fiords, where she presented a constant threat to Allied shipping. In October of 1942 the *Tirpitz* was spotted in Asen Fiord by a Norwegian sailor, Leif Larson, who had joined the British fighting forces. The British navy decided to go in after the *Tirpitz*. Because there were so many anti-submarine nets protecting the giant ship, they used a pair of sea horses or chariots. Two of these were tied to the bottom of a fishing boat disguised as a Norwegian vessel. Six charioteers, or frogmen, were hidden under the fishing tackle below decks. When the vessel, under Larson's command, came within striking distance, four of the frogmen were to mount their human torpedoes. Then they would set off below water for the target.

When only ten miles from the *Tirpitz*, both chariots were torn away by a storm and the fishing boat had to be sunk. One charioteer was caught by the Germans and shot as a spy. The rest of the men, including Larson and his crew, managed to reach safety in Sweden.

Almost a year later, in September of 1943, the British tried again. This time they attacked the *Tirpitz* with midget subs known as X-craft, released like minnows from mother submarines. Six of these midgets started on the expedition to Kaal Fiord, where the *Tirpitz* was now hiding. Because of bad weather and mechanical difficulties, only three of them actually managed to enter the fiord. They got past the anti-submarine nets and edged toward the *Tirpitz* in the black water. The *X-6* crept under the monster's belly and dropped her two huge charges to the bottom. The Germans saw the midget emerge, and fired at her. The British crew scuttled their craft and tried to swim away, but all four were captured.

The German officers were sure that limpet mines had been attached to the keel of their battleship. They sent down two suicidally brave divers to try to save the *Tirpitz*. But shortly afterward a tremendous kick hit the ship from below. On deck, both the German officers and their British prisoners were thrown on their faces. As a survivor later reported, the battleship "leaped a man's height in the air. When it settled, all three main engines and all lighting equipment was smashed."

Unknown to the captured crew, another midget, *X-7*, had also succeeded in scraping along under the *Tirpitz*' hull. There it released two more big eggs and slipped away. The 40,000-ton warship had actually been lifted up by eight tons of amatol, all bursting simultaneously on the sea's floor. All that saved the *Tirpitz* from complete destruction was the captain's last-minute order to pull on her cables, thus shifting her position slightly. *Tirpitz* was so badly shattered inside that she could not leave the fiord for another year. By the time repairs had been made, aircraft from a carrier found her and pounded her with bombs. And in November of 1944, more bombs from the R.A.F. sealed her death warrant. No longer was she a threat to Allied shipping.

9. JAPAN'S SUBMARINES ATTACK AMERICA

The Nazi conquest of France and the Netherlands in 1940 placed their weak Asiatic colonies within easy grasp of the Japanese, allies of Germany. For ten years the Japanese had been conquering the coastal regions of China. And they had all but cut off China by the time the German war machine rolled over western Europe. Now the Japanese—poor in raw materials—were eager to seize the rich supplies of rubber, rice and oil to the south. The Dutch East Indies, French Indo-China and even British Malaya and Burma seemed ready for conquest—except for the threat of defense by the United States.

The bases of the powerful United States Navy extended from the continental United States across the Pacific to the Philippines like a rifle aimed at the lines of future Japanese expansion. These powerful American defenses had to be struck down before the Japanese could reach south of China.

On December 7, 1941, some twenty-five long-range Japanese submarines pushed on miles ahead of a Japanese fleet that was sneaking toward Hawaii in a mantle of fog. Five of them carried midget submarines on their decks. Each midget had a crew of two and carried two torpedoes. Even when their mother submarine was submerged, the midget craft could be launched under water. Their job was to creep through the American nets at Pearl Harbor, designed to keep out larger submarines. After a surprise attack on the American ships by Japanese carrier-based airplanes, the midget subs were to finish off any survivors.

The mission spelled glory, but perhaps death, too. The men were ready for both. Admiral Yamamoto, the commander of the Japanese fleets, had predicted, "If our men get inside Pearl Harbor, they can never return."

He was right. Only one midget managed to penetrate the boom and nets. It released both its torpedoes before it was sunk, but they caused little damage. A second midget was probably sunk near the entrance to the harbor. A third one grounded and was captured, giving the American admirals an early peek at a secret weapon. None of the five returned to its mother submarine.

For the next four years the Japanese admirals scattered their ideas on dozens of different types of submarines. They built all sizes, from fatal midgets up to three huge 3500-tonners that were years ahead of their time. These had on deck large cylindrical hangars which could hold three tiny seaplanes. The Japanese even had two scow submarines, without engines, intended to be towed under water as gliders are towed by planes. What the Japanese did not have was a foolproof, workhorse submarine that could creep beneath the scores of American destroyers, destroyer escorts and submarines, and sink American sea supply in the Pacific.

Desperate at the failure of their torpedoes, the Japanese admirals built an explosive warhead into their midgets. They converted them into suicidal torpedoes called Kaitens. Just as the Japanese Kamikaze or suicide planes were ordered to dive into American ships, the Kaitens were ordered to steer themselves at their targets at a speed of sixteen knots.

The Kaitens had an ejector device that could be used to throw the pilots into the sea during the last fifty yards before the strike. But the submariners usually chose to ride to death bravely. Many carried smudged photos of Kaiten sailors already lost in action. These inspired them to seek a similar death.

In spite of their pilots' sacrifices, the Kaitens somehow failed. Often they were left behind by their mother submarines and lost. They were too slow to trail a convoy by themselves and had to lie in wait. And they were incapable of changing attack. The Kaitens could not be improved for a simple reason. They never came back to tell their story of what had gone wrong.

A Kaiten pilot, getting ready to attack the American fleet off Guam, wrote proudly in his diary: "Only twenty-two years of life, and now it is like a dream. The meaning of life will be shown today." But the veteran commander of the mother submarine that launched him wrote sadly in his last log, "A single radar set would be of more value than a hundred submarines."

At night and in fog, radar serves as the eyes of a submarine. The only radar the Japanese had was borrowed from the Germans, who were themselves behind in design. Other Japanese detection equipment was poor, and little effort was made to give ears to the semi-blind submarines.

But the most serious error of the Japanese was their failure to imitate the tactics of the British, the besieged island power of the Atlantic. They never really developed sub-hunting submarines. Japanese submarines, as at Pearl Harbor, operated mainly as scouts in support of their own surface fleet. Only rarely were they to be found any great distance from the ships they were to accompany. A submarine is an offensive weapon, but Japan tried to use them defensively. As a result they had only minor effect upon the great troop and materiel shipments sent by the United States across the Pacific. Their few long-range submarines seldom carried torpedoes against the Americans. Instead they became underwater grocery stores, unloading help by night on lonely beaches. They were too busy running rice and guns to their isolated garrisons to attack American submarines as savagely as the British submarines attacked German U-boats.

Even so, the Japanese sharks were able to strike death to the American carriers *Wasp* and *Yorktown*. And when the war was all but over, they sank the battleship *North Carolina* and the cruiser *Indianapolis*, taking the lives of 883 men—their last strokes in a losing war.

10. THE FIRST WAR FOR AMERICAN SUBMARINES

When Japan struck in the Pacific, the United States submarine force was untested. In World War I American submarines patrolled out of Ireland and the Azores, but found almost no targets.

At the time of the Japanese attack, the United States had only fifty-one submarines in the Pacific. They were mostly 312-foot giants carrying twenty-four torpedoes, and they were able to race twenty knots on the surface. At bases in the Philippine Islands there were twenty-three fleet type submarines, plus six creaky old S-boats from the early thirties. These were 219 feet long and carried only 10 torpedoes. But this small force was in readiness. Within hours after receiving orders for action, United States submarines were patrolling the Pacific, seeking out Japanese targets.

Only nine days after the Pearl Harbor attack, a

fat Japanese transport off Hainan Island steamed into the periscope sights of Lieutenant Commander Chester Smith, skipper of the *Swordfish*. Small and studious, Smith wore glasses and spoke in a low voice, but his aim was true. He fired three torpedoes. The transport, *Atsutusan Maru*, burst into flame, tipped up her stern, and slid under. This was the first confirmed sinking of an enemy ship by an American submarine during the war.

The American submariners grew bolder. They crept close to the Japanese shipping lanes and even to the coast of Japan itself. The *Pollack*, in January, 1942, sank a freighter outside Tokyo Bay.

Other American submarines cruised the Pacific, picking off troop and supply ships destined for enemy garrisons. Japanese garrisons stretched out over thousands of miles in the Pacific, from the China coast to the Marshall Islands and from the chilly Aleutians to the steaming tropics of Malaya. The spreading Japanese Empire seemed an easy target for any country with an efficient submarine fighting force. And the United States had good submarines.

The Americans settled early on a one-class fleet of new submarines. Like the Germans, they concentrated on building boats of the same basic size. They turned these out at top speed and with little change throughout the war. The *Gato* was their model. *Gato* was 311 feet, 9 inches long and could make 20 knots on the surface. Submerged and running on batteries, she could flee for an hour at eleven knots, or creep off at a man's walking speed for a whole day.

This work-horse submarine had ten torpedo tubes for shooting, and stowage for twenty-four torpedoes. It cost $7,000,000 and required 336 days to build. The crews were usually made up of eight officers and seventy-two men. They often stayed out longer than the German U-boat crews— from forty-five to sixty days. This submarine, however, did have a weakness. It was unsafe in a dive below 400 feet, where water pressure was 12 tons per square foot. Nevertheless, some Gatos dived deeper, where their joints "wept" sea water.

American submariners soon learned the capabilities of their Gatos. They were quick to improvise tricky uses of radar and periscope in attack, and to learn how to escape afterward from the bombs of a stubborn and imaginative enemy.

Early in 1943, *Growler*, with Commander Howard Gilmore at the eyepiece, was caught by two crisscrossing Japanese destroyers. The destroyers drove him under and depth-charged viciously. Green water poured through her leaks at fifteen gallons a minute, flooding her forward torpedo room. She stayed down all day, using her pumps in cautious gasps. Night came and she had to surface. At one in the morning Gilmore, two officers, the quartermaster and three sailors were on the bridge, peering through the woolly mist curling on the surface.

A Japanese gunboat, waiting beyond the fog for *Growler* to come up, spotted her. The gunboat opened up her engines and raced at the sub. The *Growler* turned and rammed her. A sharp-eyed Japanese seaman with a machine gun barking in his hand swept the *Growler's* bridge at point-blank range.

Gilmore was wounded. An ensign was killed. "Clear the bridge!" ordered Gilmore.

One officer, two lookouts and the quartermaster dragged themselves through the hatch. Gilmore alone remained above. The men, aching to dive, heard bullets clattering on the metal. For the submarine to remain surfaced was suicide.

Still no word came down the open hatch from the captain above. Why was he silent? Were they waiting for the orders of a man fallen overboard, or dead? Then came Gilmore's faltering voice, clear through the intercom: "Take her down."

They couldn't leave their captain. They waited. Water poured through the open hatch. The conning tower was a rising lake. Still the second officer waited and waited. The water flooded higher, and bullets continued to clatter outside. They must either obey his command or lose the lives of all. In a whisper the order was given to secure the hatch.

Growler dived. Gilmore was swept away. The submarine crept home with her nose bent like a beaten boxer's. But after repairs her crew took her into battle again.

The United States had developed a battle-hardy submarine, and the lifelines of the Japanese Empire were vulnerable. But could American submarines strangle Japan? Could they succeed in starving out a stubborn island people when the far more experienced U-boat fleet was failing to defeat the British people the same way?

It soon became clear that the answer was, *"No, not unless we get better torpedoes."* The American submarine performed well, but its torpedo was poor. Often the "fish" ran too deep. What was worse, sometimes torpedoes struck the enemy ships but failed to explode. Even the boasted new torpedoes with magnetic warheads exploded short of the target or refused to go off. They were supposed to explode automatically on passing under the metal hull of any ship.

The submariners were furious. "Design us a boat hook," Rear Admiral Charles Lockwood suggested to officials in Washington, "so we can rip the plates off their sides!" One submarine, in desperation, even sank a Japanese ship by punching a hole in her side with a dud torpedo.

Washington officials remained hard to convince. In the early months of the war few of the submariners were experienced in firing torpedoes. And as the underwater fleet expanded, the proportion of real torpedo experts continued to be small. Was the fault with the submarine crews?

A gigantic 19,000-ton Japanese ship finally

ended the duel of words between Lockwood at Pearl Harbor and the Bureau of Ordnance in Washington. The *Tonan Maru No. 3* was caught off Truk by the submarine *Tinosa* on July 24, 1943. Not one or two, but *eleven*, torpedoes were shot at the converted mother ship for whaling vessels.

It was torture for both the gunners and the target. The Japanese sailors, frightened, ran helplessly around the decks, seeing each deadly torpedo wake. A half-mile away, his jaw locked, his eye at the periscope, the submarine captain, Lieutenant Commander Dan Daspit, said little but "Fire!" and "Load!" His face was grim. He was getting the proof he needed.

Of the eleven torpedoes released, only three exploded. And these three explosions came not from head-on hits but from glancing blows that struck at an angle. Cowering while eight of the torpedoes clanged harmlessly against the sides of their ship, the Japanese sailors escaped what had seemed to be a certain death. As a final humiliation, the colossal whale factory, its paint scratched by harmless hits, was towed to safety despite its three holes.

What was wrong? The exploder in the nose of the torpedoes was obviously a misfit freak. In order to set off the 685 pounds of TNT it had to hit foul and sideways. A perfect shot, striking head on, would not go off.

All over the Pacific the commanders of the scattered submarines received new radio orders that made them blink and scratch their heads. The gist of the instructions was: avoid all straight hits. If they saw an easy shot, they were to turn it into a difficult angle before shooting. Had the admirals ashore gone crazy?

They had, almost. Lockwood and Captain C. B. Momsen sent the submarine *Muskallunge* off the tiny Hawaiian island of Kahoolawe to shoot three torpedoes from different angles at its rocky cliffs. Two torpedoes burst against the rocky bluffs, but one struck and sank without an explosion. Men on the testing team had to swim down in fifty-five feet of water, find the dud, and haul it up, all the time expecting it to explode. Then the dud had to be taken apart. After three long weeks of testing, they discovered what was wrong with the small $630 exploder. And they finally found out by taking warheads to the top of a "cherry-picker" crane and dropping them like coconuts onto a steel plate.

By the second half of 1943, the kinks had been taken out of the firing mechanisms, and the new Mark 18 electric torpedo had been put to use. The American submarines became much more deadly.

The Americans, of course, knew all about the wolf-pack methods used by the Germans. They decided to adapt the U-boat tactics to the small, fast Japanese convoys. Because the Japanese rarely ran more than ten ships together, the American wolf packs used only four submarines instead of the fifteen or twenty gathered by the Germans against the huge Atlantic convoys. Four Gato-type submarines were enough to do the job in the Pacific.

In the many narrow channels between the Pacific Islands, especially off the Asiatic coast, the Americans had favorite hunting places. Most of these had code names such as "Convoy College," "Hit Parade," "The Speedway" and "Maru Morgue." The most dangerous hunting, however, was in the foggy, cold channels of northern Japan. Here traffic was light, visibility poor, currents strong and tricky, and mine fields thick and changeable.

The richest hunting was along the deeper passages between the Chinese coast and the islands of Formosa and the Philippines. These channels were too wide or too busy to mine, or were buoyed, like Formosa Channel. Here fat Japanese transports heavy with soldiers, tanks, artillery and vehicles plowed south. On the return trip the same ships were hull-deep with rice, oil, rubber and iron.

Usually luck determined the size of a submarine's prize. And frequently luck seemed to determine the fate of a submarine as well. Some were "lucky boats," even when their first patrols did badly.

The Squalus, for example, had sunk in 240 feet of water off Portsmouth, New Hampshire, before the war started. Her sister, *Sculpin,* found her. A rescue chamber was lowered, but only 33 of her men were saved. The *Squalus* was raised, refitted for duty and renamed *Sailfish.* But nobody wanted to serve on her. She was supposed to be "haunted."

When *Sailfish* went to war, however, a strange thing happened. Other submarines set out to patrol Japanese waters and never returned, but *Sailfish* kept coming home. Soon the theory of her being haunted changed. She became a "lucky boat." It was said that having been sunk already, she could never be sunk again.

On her tenth patrol in December, 1943, *Sailfish* proved her luck. After twilight she surfaced in a storm. "Tremendous seas, 40-50 knot wind, driving rain and visibility from zero to 500 yards," Lieutenant Commander Bob Ward wrote in his log.

Feeding up his batteries at midnight in these wild seas, Ward saw two big pips on his radar. He edged closer, aiming at one dim monster. He fired four shots from a mile and a quarter through the whipping seas. The first and last torpedo hit. A destroyer turned after him. He dived, twisted away, and surfaced again. He had to make sure he had done a thorough job on whatever it was he had hit.

Gradually Ward stole up on the shadowy form, then fired three more torpedoes. "The first hit," he wrote, "looked like a momentary puff of fire.

The second hit looked like and sounded on our bridge like a battleship firing a broadside—even with the locomotive rumble so characteristic of 16-inch shells."

Sailfish then submerged and waited for dawn, two hours away. By the sun's first light, Ward saw that he had stopped a 20,000-ton aircraft carrier, *Chuyo*. From his unsteady periscope, he could see "many planes on deck forward and enough people on deck aft to populate a fair-sized village." From the numbers on deck he assumed that they were preparing to abandon ship. Reassured, he fired two more torpedoes at a distance of a mile. Both hit. He dived. There were "exceptionally loud breaking up noises." He lifted his periscope to search for destroyers, but was scared under by a big cruiser which tore at him.

Unknown to Ward the carrier *Chuyo* carried a terrible secret in her hold. Had he known, he might not have shot those last two torpedoes. Locked in the *Chuyo's* brig were twenty-one submariners—American prisoners. And they came from that very sister submarine, the *Sculpin*, which had once discovered Ward's submarine helpless on the bottom near Portsmouth's Isle of Shoals.

These twenty-one prisoners from the *Sculpin* had their own story—a story that was pieced together only after the end of the war.

In November, 1943, *Sculpin*, commanded by Commander Fred Connaway, was heading for the great Japanese naval base at Truk. Aboard her, Captain John Cromwell, an American wolf-pack commander, was traveling with secret orders he had memorized, then destroyed. These orders had to do with the coming American fleet attack on the Gilbert Islands. They concerned the special wolf-pack methods to be used if Japanese naval forces came out from Truk to intervene.

Sculpin was trailing a convoy when an enemy destroyer sighted her. She dived. Shattering explosions caused her depth gauge to fail. Then a squall blew up, and *Sculpin* was able to rise and fix the damage behind the curtains of gray rain. But the rain eased off. Another destroyer saw her and charged. This time *Sculpin* dropped to 400 feet, her seams bleeding water. Her batteries were exhausted. Choosing a fight to death, hoping to save some of his men, Connaway issued his orders. "Surface! Battle stations! Gun action!"

Sculpin broke water, and her men manned the

3-inch gun. A Japanese destroyer stood off at a safe distance and threw 5-inch shells until Connaway and his gun crew were killed. "Abandon ship!" ordered Lieutenant George Brown.

But Captain Cromwell refused to use his life jacket. Though he had no telltale written orders, he did not trust his physical strength against Japanese tortures. "Sorry, Brown, I can't go with you," he said firmly. "I know too much." With a dozen other men trapped inside, including Ensign C. G. Smith, Jr. who also refused to leave, he voluntarily "rode down" with the *Sculpin*. In the tradition of the bravest submarine captains, he chose death rather than to risk dishonor.

The United States submarine force in the Pacific gradually expanded. Gato-type craft came off the assembly lines with regularity, and the Navy managed to produce well-trained submariners to man them—even during the darkest days of the war in the Pacific. While submarines were helping to turn the tide for America in the Pacific, U-boats were gradually becoming less important as a German weapon in the Atlantic.

11. THE U-BOATS ON DEFENSE

During the last years of U-boat warfare, the new German submarine captains averaged only 21 years of age. To encourage them, Admiral Doenitz used to show them a painting on his wall jokingly called "Fleet Review in 1955." It portrayed only sea gulls flying over rough waves, with no ships in sight. The whole navy was under water. This was the Admiral's way of showing his young commanders that they were on the side of the future. If they couldn't dive or fly they would be dead, Doenitz insisted. The surface waters, sandwiched between aircraft and submarines, would be intolerably dangerous.

Earlier in the war Admiral Doenitz' prediction seemed to be right. Most sinkings were made by bold night attacks on the surface, with U-boats using their Diesel-engine speed to attack, their slow batteries only to escape under water. In 1942 more than 1500 Allied ships were sunk. Scarcely a torpedo missed. For the loss of only 85 submarines, 8,245,000 tons of Allied shipping vanished.

In the end, though, things did not turn out as Doenitz' painting predicted. The U-boats were driven to hide under the waves, while their enemies remained on top.

The U-boat had two basic weaknesses. It had a slow rate of escape under water, and it was deaf to sounds astern.

After torpedoing a ship and diving to escape destroyers, the U-boat crept away at barely four knots. Her crew hoped to make their batteries last a full 30 hours—that is, more than 120 miles. They could hear the whizzing sounds of destroyers searching to right, left and ahead. But astern, the U-boat's own propellers drowned out or garbled the noises of pursuing killers.

To exploit this deafness, British destroyers worked out a method of double pursuit. A fake pursuer would hang back a half-mile behind the escaping U-boat's tail. The destroyer was near enough to hear the submarine creeping away, but far enough away not to be heard by the U-boat's propeller-deafened ears. She would trail the

U-boat at its own speed, not trying to overtake it. While creeping along behind the submarine, this destroyer with silently blinking lamp, would call on a second destroyer to take the same position, beside her.

The second destroyer, with her "pinging" sound gear silent to keep the U-boat unaware, would then move up slowly ahead of the first destroyer. The first destroyer, pinging far astern on the U-boat, continued to blink directions silently to the second destroyer—the real hunter. "Go right a little. Now go left." To avoid giving alarm, the killer destroyer would creep ahead at a speed that was only one knot faster than the escaping U-boat. The U-boat might hear the searching pings of the first destroyer far astern, but not the motor of the phantom silently overtaking her.

At the moment when the killer's softly whirring screws took her directly over the U-boat, she received the winking signal from her partner, "Drop DCs!" Then out flew her depth charges and down they plunged on the unsuspecting U-boat. The sea went wild with explosions. And soon up came oil, cork and other floatable scraps from the shattered victim.

The Americans—and the Japanese—also used the twin hunter system. But with them the silent hunter followed behind the submarine, while the "pinger" sent echoes from off the quarter of the fugitive.

To hide from the reaching fingers of asdic or sonar, U-boats liked the warm Gulf Stream. There the pings of the destroyers bounced off the scales of the densely packed schools of fish as if they were the metal plates of a U-boat. Only an experienced listener could detect a mushy sound. In the Arctic the mixture of currents—icy, moderate and warmish—made for layers of different density. And even in the Pacific the pinging signals of the surface hunters bounced back like a rubber ball from layers as deep as 300 feet, or were bent so that they gave a false direction. In the icy Atlantic the U-boat could find a protective blanket 160 feet down.

At first U-boats worried mainly about depth charges. These were 600-pound "ashcans" of high explosive dumped overboard in intricate patterns from a destroyer's stern. Although they were more powerful than those used in the First World War, they had changed little. To crush a submarine's plates, a depth charge had to burst within thirty feet of the underwater craft. But they could never be planted except by the aid of sound, which was never entirely accurate.

In one way, the old-fashioned depth charges actually helped the U-boats. They always churned up the waters into a noisy foam of bubbles and gurgles. Effective sound-tracking was impossible until quiet returned. This could take as much as fifteen minutes. Meanwhile, under the sizzling cover of the noisy explosions, a bold U-boat commander could sneak away. He could speed a half-mile in any direction and then silence his motors again when the bubbling stopped.

To offset this problem, the British devised a weapon the U-boats learned to hate. It was called the "hedgehog." The hedgehog was put to use during the dark days of 1942. Unlike depth charges, the new weapon was silent and fast. It consisted of a giant fistful of tiny projectiles shaped like potato mashers. The pursuing destroyer, instead of blindly dropping slow, noisy depth charges, threw this deadly circle of explosive quills 250 yards ahead toward the area where the U-boat had been heard. The quills sank silently, a cloud of little projectiles.

If one quill touched a U-boat anywhere, it blew a hole in her plates, flooding her fatally. If none touched, the pursuing destroyer could still drop her depth charges. By these two attacks—the silent and the noisy—the U-boat had two chances of being killed, instead of one.

The following year things began to go wrong for the U-boats in the Bay of Biscay, their front door to the Atlantic. The U-boats had been in the habit of surfacing at night to recharge their tired batteries. Their commanders felt protected by "Metox," their warning radar. This clever gadget gave them notice whenever radar on an Allied ship was fingering their profile, anywhere up to a distance of ten miles. The U-boat could dive before being attacked.

But suddenly Metox did not seem to work. Out of the safe black night, an overhead light would suddenly gleam on the U-boat's decks. Immediately aerial bombs came raining down. The lookouts piled into the hatch, and the U-boats dived to come up again miles away, their batteries more tired than ever. Again there would be the lights, the bombs, the dive.

It was clear that the British were spotting the

U-boats from the air. But how? Admiral Doenitz had a terrible suspicion. Perhaps Metox itself was betraying them. Perhaps this radar detector was itself putting out some telltale beam that was giving away the U-boat's location.

He gave orders for secret tests. A Metox was operated on a U-boat in safe home waters while a German bomber circled overhead. Sure enough, the plane picked up the beam from Metox. Doenitz flashed a signal to all U-boats at sea, "Stop using Metox!"

The U-boats obeyed, but in vain. They still suffered from surprise attacks by air at night. In the single fearful month of April, 1943, Doenitz lost forty-three submarines. The tide was turning against the U-boats.

On their way to the mid-Atlantic hunting grounds, the U-boats could no longer poke along, submerged, on batteries by day and race at top speed, surfaced, on Diesel engines at night. They now had to drag along at the speed of a sailboat both day and night. They came home at the same wasteful pace, crawling through the zone of night-seeing aircraft. When could a U-boat recharge her batteries on the surface if nights were as dangerous as days? Without batteries a U-boat could not operate submerged. Yet she must. What was the British secret eye?

Too late, the U-boat engineers finally got the answer. It came from two British bombers that crashed, far apart, on raids deep into Germany. From the wrecks the Germans pieced together the halves of the secret British radar bombsight that was killing submarines.

It was a miraculous receiver called a Braun tube. It operated on radio waves only 10 centimeters long, the length of a man's hand. These tiny waves had been studied by German radar experts earlier, but they had been discarded as useless. They detected only objects near at hand, fully within sight. At that time the Germans were seeking radar which would work at a greater distance. They overlooked the fact that these tiny waves, though short, were much harder to detect.

It was a fatal error, for the bombsights made Metox useless. By the time the U-boats caught on, their advanced Atlantic bases were already in danger. Years later Admiral Doenitz said that radar, next to the atomic bomb, was the most decisive weapon of the war.

The U-boat wolf-pack technique of attack was also proving to have a weakness. After sighting a convoy, the scouting U-boat had to send a warning to Doenitz, who would choose a meeting place for the U-boat wolf pack. These warning calls usually began with the letter B. The Allied radio operators, overhearing, called them "B-bars." The B-bars, unfortunately, gave away the location of the submarine. A careful listener could even tell if the signal came from a wet or dry antenna. Thus he knew whether or not the U-boat had just surfaced.

By knowing the location of the scouting U-boat, the Allied convoy commander could change course. It became much harder for the wolf pack to attack before the hurrying ships reached the friendly umbrella of offshore bombers with their terrible all-night cats' eyes.

The increasing skill of British anti-submarine warfare permitted a steady stream of men, arms and other necessities to flow from North America across the Atlantic. But the U-boat was not yet defeated. The German submarines fought harder than ever to drown American forces and supplies en route to Europe and Africa. By autumn of

1943, German engineers had developed the acoustic torpedo with "ears" tuned to a ship's propeller. When this torpedo, which could race at forty-five knots, approached its target it would suddenly "hear" the thrashing propellers. It would immediately swerve and dart toward them.

These listening torpedoes made it unnecessary for the U-boat to plan for a costly attack at the broad side of a ship, using three or four fish. Instead, a single torpedo, fired safely from several miles astern, made the kill cleanly, safely and cheaply. This weapon was called GNAT by the British and "Zaunkönig" (Wren) by its German inventors.

To throw off the GNATS, the freighters learned to stop all engines and call on the destroyers to hunt the U-boat. But this was dangerous because stopping broke up the convoy. It made each ship a sitting duck, for stopping could not make the ship invisible. In addition, it wasn't sure. The U-boats developed a torpedo so sharp of hearing that it could detect even the minor noises of a stopped ship.

So the British devised a better defense. When entering U-boat waters, ships put out a noise maker which screamed loudly and was towed astern. These "Foxers" drew in the torpedoes and caused them to burst in empty water. The trick had a weakness, however. The Foxers made so much racket that a prowling U-boat could not be heard astern. The ships ended up with the same weakness as U-boats: deafness to the enemy.

Harassed by radar-equipped planes in the air, and out-foxed by British sea defenses, the U-boat faced still another torture—the sonar buoy. Dropped in the water where a submerged U-boat was playing dead, this floating sentinel listened for the first whir of the submarine's motors. The sonar buoy did not have to circle around as the hunting destroyers had done in the past. Instead it floated on the surface above the hidden U-boat. At the first furtive turn of the submarine's screws, the sonar buoy howled a warning that brought the savage destroyers racing back, dumping charges on all sides.

Despite all these new techniques of destruction and defense, combats still frequently took place in old-fashioned style. The famous battle fought between *U-66* and the American destroyer *Buckley* in May, 1944, was settled hand to hand and man to man.

U-66 was waiting in mid-Atlantic for her "milch cow" or supply submarine. A carrier plane sighted her at three on a moonlit morning. To warn her mother submarine *U-66* sent up three red lights. She was caught in a moonlit path by the *Buckley*, which had raced in from twenty miles away.

A three-inch shell cracked *U-66*'s conning tower. She could not dive, so she tried to run away on the surface. They raced along, destroyer and submarine, scarcely a hundred feet apart, shooting at each other as they tore along. Suddenly Lieutenant Commander Abel on the *Buckley* swung over his helm, aiming to cut in and knife the sub in two.

At a 35-knot speed the *Buckley* went right up over the hull of the *U-66*. The vessels were like two crossed skis. The U-boat men poured out of the hatches onto the slippery deck, guns in hand. From their own sinking deck they climbed up the destroyer's sides, keeping up a heavy fire with revolvers and submachine guns.

Over the *Buckley's* loud-speaker rang out the old, almost forgotten cry of much earlier wars, "Stand by to repel boarders!" But with what? The crew of the destroyer searched frantically in their lockers for little-used or forgotten revolvers. Was a submarine going to capture a destroyer?

The first Germans to advance down the *Buckley's* foredeck were met by a barrage of empty shell cases, cans and coffee mugs. The destroyer by now had slipped off the submarine's deck, so that the U-boat was on the *Buckley's* port side. The submarine was flooding but still trying to ram.

Just in time the Americans remembered a store of grenades. Few of the sailors had ever seen grenades, a soldier's weapon. Fewer still had ever used them. But the deadly pineapples were passed up the hatch. The "swabs" scarcely knew how to work the timer's catch on the grenades. But from baseball practice they knew how to throw them.

A grenade rolled down the hatch of *U-66*. Then another curved through the air and landed neatly in the broken conning tower. After a flash of fire, the bridge of *U-66* was sprawling with bodies. Then the hatch closed, and the U-boat broke away and dived. She was never seen again. But the bravest of the Germans—the thirty-six who survived the storming of the *Buckley*—became the prisoners of the destroyer's crew.

The fat-bellied German "milch cows," which

carried 1,720 tons of Diesel oil, made big targets for the underwater fingers of sound that were always groping for them. The Germans had developed these supply subs for their wolf packs after British tactics made it both risky and slow for the U-boats to cross the Bay of Biscay. The German subs relied heavily on their cows during the last two years of the war. Whenever one of these supply giants was sunk, a whole wolf pack went idle until another could come out.

But the cows were clever when it came to deep diving. The *U-490*, a supply submarine caught off the Azores by hunter-killers, dived to the unbelievable depth of 700 feet. After seventeen hours at this terrible depth, unable to make repairs, the captain brought up the leaking *U-490*. The destroyers found her and pounded her with shells till she plunged forever, leaving sixty gas-dazed, exhausted men in the icy water.

As the U-boats passed through the unsafe waters of Biscay less frequently, Allied patrols went farther afield to seek them out. Since the U-boats could no longer spend the night safely charging batteries on the surface of the Atlantic, Admiral Doenitz intensified work on the snorkel, or snout. U-boats were fitted with a long, collapsible tube so they could travel submerged on their Diesel engines instead of their batteries. This snorkel was a kind of long breathing tube to provide air for the engines under water. Intake and exhaust valves were contained in a device that took in a constant supply of air. The snorkel was based on an ancient principle which had been adapted to submarines before. Even Bushnell had a primitive kind of snorkel on the *Turtle*.

Submerged except for these metal nostrils, the U-boats could recharge their batteries under water at night with much less danger than when their whole profile was exposed. Their speed submerged remained slow, but not as slow as it would have been on batteries. To soften or throw off radar waves, the protruding nostrils were covered with soft rubber paint. By day, however, the big pipes of the snorkel left such a heavy wake in the water that it was easily noticeable from the air.

Even by night a U-boat with radar equipment and periscope submerged and only her snorkel showing might be raked by highly sensitive radar from sea or sky without knowing danger was near. The Germans, therefore, attached onto the snout an extra warning device called "Naxos."

It warned the submerged commander if his snorkel was being fingered by the hostile radar of a destroyer or plane. Then he could dive.

New magic torpedoes that could be launched from as far down as 160 feet helped U-boat commanders to realize an old dream of submariners. They could now conceal the direction from which their torpedoes were fired. The U-boat could take aim, dive, and then fire when she was halfway toward the safety of the depths. The new torpedoes no longer darted straight for the ship's propellers and the noisy Foxers which dragged behind. Instead, they ran in deceptive curves and even zigzags.

As the Germans forged ahead with new plans to improve their underwater fleet, Allied naval men became extremely eager to get a look at the new German weapons. Captain Daniel V. Gallery of the United States Navy was consumed with the ambition, impossible as it seemed, of trapping an entire U-boat alive, complete with crew, radio codes and engineering secrets. In June, 1944, after sighting a U-boat, he flashed an order to his escorts that seemed laughable: "Draw up plans and organize a party to board, capture and take sub in tow if opportunity arises."

His victim was the *U-505*, a hard-luck submarine whose first captain had shot himself during a depth-charge attack. Captain Gallery's scouting planes got on the trail of the *U-505* off the bulge of Africa. They needled the waves around her with bullets. Then they pulled in the destroyers, which hammered the sea around the U-boat with a dozen 600-pound depth charges.

Under this torture *U-505* broke surface. Her commander, Harald Lange, swung her tail around to kick off the torpedoes from his stern tubes. Three destroyers peppered her bridge, not with the tearing 3-inch shells, but with machine-gun fire planned to kill her officers.

"Abandon ship and scuttle her," Lange ordered. A moment later, machine-gun bullets smashed his legs and deck splinters tore open his face. He fainted, bleeding on the deck.

The *U-505's* engines were still burning as the crewmen jumped overboard. When about fifty Germans were splashing in the water, Gallery's destroyer-flotilla leader, Commander F. S. Hall, blinked him a joyful signal: "We are going to board. Away boarding parties. Lower all whaleboats."

Led by an ex-submariner, Lieutenant A. G.

David, the Americans stormed up *U-505's* wave-washed side. At the battered bridge they stepped over a dead gunner's mate, cut down before he could reach the deck gun. The hatch was closed and stuck. They pulled a German out of the water, ordered him to open it, then pushed him back for safe-keeping. Waves were already washing over the tilting deck. The sailors raced below and spun the sea cocks closed.

Every U-boat, the Americans knew, had exactly fourteen five-pound packages of TNT fixed all over the inside of the hull. The time fuses were supposed to be started by a sinking crew as soon as the lead-weighted codebooks were thrown overboard. David's men found thirteen of the charges, but not the fourteenth.

Only after *U-505* had been towed 2500 miles to Bermuda, three weeks later, was the hiding place of Number 14 discovered. The wounded commanding officer, who had been fished out of the water, kept repeating, "I will be punished for this." His nervousness was natural. His codebooks, his ciphering machine, and the general system by which the U-boats changed their code every two weeks, all fell into American hands.

It still seemed, however, that for each U-boat

secret the Allies could capture, the Germans could create a new one. They managed to think up these new submarine ideas in spite of the fact that German armies were being rolled back on all fronts.

Even after losing their Atlantic bases in France, the U-boat men refused to give up. They continued to fight in the North Sea with midget submarines. The Nazi submariners were just getting used to midgets when the surrender came. Although they still had more than 500 of their various midget models on hand, there was no longer a Fatherland to keep the boats supplied.

The U-boat men, in the Second World War as in the First, felt that the other services had lost the war. They considered themselves still unbeaten. By the time of surrender they had lost 781 U-boats—655 in battle—out of 1,159 commissioned. According to Prime Minister Winston Churchill they had sunk 20,448,074 tons. According to the different tonnage values of America's Admiral Ernest J. King, the figure was 23,351,000 tons—twice as much as U-boats had sunk in the first war. The British, starting with 58 submarines, raised their fleet to 219, but lost 74 of them.

When Germany surrendered, the Germans were still technically the master submariners of the world. They had 120 new Diesel-electric submarines ready for sea, with 86 trained crews. By far the fastest in the world, these ships could do 15.6 knots surfaced and 17 knots below. This was the first submarine in history to be more efficient under the waves than on surface. Besides these work horses, Doenitz had eight new Walther types that burned a mixture of hydrogen peroxide, oil and steam and could speed along for six hours at twenty-five knots submerged—faster than the fastest American submarines could travel on the surface. But the Admiral had lost two vital zones— the surface above his U-boats and the bases behind them.

Of her deep-water U-boats Germany surrendered 156, but scuttled 221. One submarine escaped to South America as a final gesture of defiance, running 66 days submerged at snorkel depth— the last record established by Doenitz' underwater fleet.

Far down in the sea, crushed in their flattened coffins, were 33,000 German officers and men, ten times as many submariners as America lost.

12. AMERICAN SUBMARINES SWEEP THE PACIFIC

After three years of fighting, American submarines in the Pacific developed a strategy new to underwater warfare. They sank the Japanese destroyers first. After these were down, it was easy to sink the convoys. This rule was a reversal of the original order to save the torpedoes for big targets like carriers and tankers.

The dangerous enemies of submarines are the savage little warships that guard the convoys—the destroyers, corvettes and frigates. These slippery waterbugs are hazardous to attack. The "safe kills" are the long, deep ships like tankers and transports. Even aircraft carriers can be considered safe if taken by surprise. The big ships are easy targets. But it is necessary to eliminate the dangerous little targets first.

Midway in the war Admiral Ernest King raised destroyers to top priority. The captain who most successfully struck at the defenders of the Japanese convoys was Sam Dealey of the *Harder*, the "torpedo-totin' Texan."

Dealey was sent on a mission to evacuate six intelligence men from Borneo. On June 6, 1944, he began to enter Sibutu Passage, which was bristling with Japanese warships. He spotted a small convoy escorted by two or three destroyers. By running on the surface, Dealey lured the 1500-ton destroyer *Minatsuki* into chasing him. "At nineteen knots we left a wake like a broad avenue five miles astern," he logged. It was a moonlit night.

When the hard-breathing destroyer was two miles away, he dived to periscope depth and swung hard to port. As the *Minatsuki* came charging on, Dealey broke water for a peep every five seconds, simulating the rhythm of breaking waves. The destroyer's lookouts missed the submarine's periscope. She roared straight on, aiming for where *Harder's* earlier dive bubbles were still popping.

Watching from a thousand yards offside, Dealey set off three torpedoes. Two struck. The *Minatsuki* split and plunged. Her depth charges blew up below, destroying the swimming Japanese sailors. Dealey surfaced, sure he would find two or three survivors. But only a burning life buoy floated on the water. There was not even a body.

Another enemy destroyer, seeing the flare and missing her comrade, pursued the *Harder*. But Dealey dived and hid under a comfortable blanket of cold water. It deflected the searching pings as a tin roof does hail.

The next day the 1700-ton destroyer *Hayanami* saw Dealey's periscope less than a mile away. Dealey logged that the Japanese "headed directly at us . . . with four tubes ready forward to fire. . . ." Dealey's bow was facing the Japanese directly. Four torpedoes were readied. The destroyer came on, weaving back and forth, "jigging," to throw off the submarine's aim.

Dealey logged: "At 650 yards, with torpedo spread of one-fourth a degree, commenced firing just as target started swinging back. Fired one-two-three in rapid succession, about five seconds interval. Number four wasn't necessary. Fifteen seconds after the first shot was fired, it struck the destroyer squarely amidships. Number two hit just aft. Number three missed ahead. Ordered right full rudder and ahead full to get clear. At range of 300 yards were rocked by terrific explosion believed to be destroyer's magazine. In less than one minute after the first hit, and nine minutes after it was sighted, the destroyer sank tail first."

Other destroyers closed in, but Dealey evaded them and reached his beach on Borneo. On June 9, while returning with the intelligence men, the *Harder* was spotted by two destroyers which zigzagged toward her. The sub fired four torpedoes, which struck when the destroyers were approaching her line of fire. Two hit the first and one the second.

The following day Dealey discovered a full fleet of "pagodas," big Japanese battleships, in formation. But a watchdog destroyer spied the feather of the *Harder's* periscope. "We're going to take a working-over anyway," said Sam, "so let's have a crack at him first."

This time *Harder* and the destroyer were roaring on a "collision course," straight at each other. Other destroyers were closing in. At 1400 yards Dealey fired three torpedoes, then snapped, "Take her down."

He was almost sunk by his victim. ". . . two torpedoes struck with a detonation far worse than depth charges. We were just passing 80 feet and were soon almost beneath the destroyer," he wrote in his log. Then came a deafening series of progressive rumblings. Either the destroyer's boilers or magazines—or both—had exploded.

The admirals could order their submarines to ambush destroyers, but a big, soft aircraft carrier remained the dream of all submariners. How else could a submarine add twenty or thirty thousand tons to its score. Aircraft carriers had an extra handicap besides their huge size. When discovered at work in daylight, launching or receiving planes, they could not zigzag. To keep an even wind flowing across their flight decks, they had to keep their bows in the wind, on a straight, easy-to-hit course. The planes were too busy landing to look for submarines.

This dream came true for a United States submarine, *Cavalla*, on her baptismal trip. On June 18, 1944, Commander H. J. Kossler saw a welcome picture in his periscope lens. *Shokaku*, 30,000 tons of costly planes, explosive bombs and inflammable gasoline hoses, was steering arrow-straight to allow her circling planes to land. At three-quarters of a mile Kossler fired six torpedoes. As the first torpedo struck, two Japanese cruisers and a destroyer ran toward the sub, pumping the sea white with depth charges. But *Cavalla* was already deep below. When she struggled up again her first radio report said:

"Hit *Shokaku*-class carrier with three out of six torpedoes. . . . Received 105 depth charges during three hour period. . . . Supersonic gear out of commission. . . . Hull induction flooded. . . . No other serious trouble. . . . Sure we can handle it. . . . Heard four terrific explosions in direction of target two-and-one-half hours after attack."

Slowly *Shokaku* sank. But often a carrier could absorb several torpedoes and still float. It was usually her nervous system of crossed gasoline lines, bombs and ammunition feeds that spread trouble. Often gases would gather in closed compartments, then suddenly blow up with a spark from a connection. Some big ships can survive torpedoes by locking off flooded compartments. But a carrier, once she starts burning in one or two places, circulates fire in her bloodstream till she sinks herself.

Just one day after the *Shokaku* was sunk, another American sub, the *Albacore*, spotted the 31,000-ton Japanese carrier *Taiho*. It was early in the morning, and the carrier was racing along at twenty-seven knots, faster than any submarine could pursue by daylight. Commander J. W. Blanchard took aim, but a destroyer cut across, spoiling his first shot. Then bad luck hit him. Something happened to his torpedo computer, and it began giving wrong numbers. Using grammar-school arithmetic, Blanchard fired six torpedoes, spread wide for error. The spread was too wide and there was only one hit. *Albacore* dived deep, with a discouraged crew cursing the computer.

Weeks later a talkative Japanese prisoner disclosed that the *Taiho* was no more. The one torpedo had struck while her planes were being filled with gas. There were inflammable fuel lines all over the deck. For six hours the leaky lines caused gases to pile up everywhere. It was impossible to ventilate all compartments. Then, from somewhere, there came a spark and a terrible flash. The enemy carrier went down with all her planes and most of her crew.

Of course submarines found more destroyers

where there were bigger targets. *Archerfish*, an American submarine dogged by hard luck, had been patrolling off Tokyo Bay for twenty-nine days. She had found nothing. Then one night at the end of November, an enormous pip, big as an island, swam onto her radar screen. It was an aircraft carrier racing along at twenty knots, with four destroyers frisking near by.

Commander J. F. Enright flashed his good news to Pearl Harbor: "Am pursuing large aircraft carrier four destroyers." Back came an answer possible only from an American submarine admiral. "Keep after him, Joe. Your picture is on the piano."

The Japanese crew aboard the destroyers had more complex things than submarines on their minds. They were running in practice formation against the powerful new engines of one of the biggest warships in the world. She was the 59,000-ton super-carrier, *Shinano*, originally intended as a battleship, but converted to a carrier. She was now on her way to a safe and secret yard for outfitting with catapults and planes.

Racing through the moonlight, from midnight to 3:00 A.M., Enright could get only nineteen knots out of his aching Diesels. But he hung on, hoping for a change of course by the carrier. Finally she did change course, and *Archerfish* was able to cut in ahead. The sub slipped down to periscope depth and waited. As the monster approached, Enright fired six torpedoes, spaced eight seconds apart.

C-R-A-N-G! His crew heard the first blow. Then *C-R-A-N-G!* again. The first two torpedoes had struck. A ball of fire climbed into the night. The nearest destroyer turned and charged for the submarine. "Take her down!" snapped Enright.

As *Archerfish* dived, with the noise of the destroyer's propellers growing ever louder, the submariners heard four more *C-R-A-N-G-S.* Every torpedo had hit. Then came a shaking rain of depth charges. *Archerfish* sank low, suffered awhile, then crept away slowly. About seven hours later the *Shinano* rolled over and sank.

The super-carrier was not only the largest warship ever sunk by a submarine, she was also the youngest, downed before a single airplane left her deck.

Victory was slowly coming over the horizon. And

it was as beautiful a sight for American submariners as an aircraft carrier filling a periscope. But the men in submarines were paying a higher price than any other seamen. And often the stories of the most valiant subs ended in tragedy.

Gudgeon was a proud submarine. She had made history, too. The Japanese submarine *I-173*, sunk by her in January, 1942, was the first enemy submarine ever sunk by a United States submarine. On her twelfth patrol the *Gudgeon* was surprised on the surface by a Japanese bomber. Her end, as the Japanese pilots reported it, was mercifully quick: "Our first bomb hit bow. Second bomb direct on bridge. Center of submarine burst. Oil pillars rose."

Although the cost of victory in the Pacific was high, its rewards were great. American submarines sank 214 Japanese warships, just under a half-million tons, and 1,152 merchant ships, nearly five million tons. About one-fiftieth of these were sunk by a single submarine, *Flasher*, under two commanders, R. I. Whitaker and G. W. Grider.

In one wild patrol Grider was caught by a Japanese destroyer. He hit her with two torpedoes, twisted away like an eel and emptied his stern tubes at a tanker. An angry destroyer pounded him under. But Grider soon sneaked a periscope peek. His would-be killer-destroyer had stopped her engines and was lying bravely alongside the flaming tanker.

After scanning this freakish double target a moment, Grider ordered four torpedoes, two deep, then two shallow. The deep pair coursed under the destroyer and blasted the tanker apart so ferociously that it blew out her fires. The shallow fish murdered the destroyer, leaving only wreckage. In one fantastic month *Flasher* sank 42,868 tons, including four tankers averaging 10,000 tons each.

Champion submarines had to take chances to keep their lead. Another American sub, *Tang*, in a short nine-month period during 1944 sank 24 ships with a total of 93,824 tons. Yet busy as she was attacking, *Tang* was even better at the humane duty of rescuing aviators. During the great air attack on Truk—April 30-May 1, 1944—Commander Richard O'Kane took the submarine dangerously close to shore by daylight. The waters were full of sharp coral heads, among which floated American fliers, shot down while bombing.

The soaked, shocked aviators, often bleeding, waved feebly for help. The Japanese shore guns were ready to blast any submarine that surfaced to help them.

Then O'Kane had an idea. He called the fliers' mother carrier by radio. The carrier sent him an umbrella of fighter planes. With the watchful fighter planes circling over the submarine, the hidden Japanese coast guns dared not shoot. *Tang* lay naked on the surface in bright sunshine, a fully exposed target. A crippled float plane from a cruiser, too broken to fly, taxied around the surface like a scooter, bringing O'Kane half-drowned fliers. Of thirty-five fliers shot down, *Tang* saved twenty-two. In all, during the war, picket submarines acting as life guards saved 504 fliers.

Of America's 288 submarines, 52 were lost, 45 of them probably in enemy action. The Japanese, meanwhile, had lost 130 submarines out of 181. A single American destroyer, *England*, sank five Japanese submarines.

An American submariner's chance of losing his life was six times greater than that of any deck-walking sailor on a surface ship. Yet the Americans were more efficient than the German masters. They sank twenty-six ships for each submarine they lost, while the Germans lost a submarine for every four ships.

Under the Pacific, in the deepest valleys of the earth, lie 374 American officers and 3,131 gallant men, submariners all.

Admiral H. G. Rickover (facing the camera) talks with Commander J. F. Calvert (left) and Neil McElroy (right), former secretary of defense.

General Dynamics Corp.

The USS *Nautilus*, world's first nuclear-powered submarine, enters New York Harbor.

Above: The *Nautilus* makes an emergency surface during a test voyage.

U. S. Navy

Top right: Crew members aboard an atomic-powered sub relax in the close quarters of their bunk room.

U. S. Navy

Bottom right: Life aboard an atomic submarine is demanding but there is no ship in the fleet where the chow is better.

U. S. Navy

As the *Nautilus* submerges to begin her historic voyage to the North Pole, Dr. Waldo K. Lyon, senior scientist (left), Comdr. W. R. Anderson (center) and Lt. Comdr. F. M. Adams watch the activity in the control room.

A single pilot in the control room of the *Nautilus* can carry out the work of three operators in a conventional sub.

A torpedoman performs a routine check on the torpedo tubes as the *Nautilus* speeds along beneath Arctic ice.

Personnel from the USS *Sargo,* third atomic sub to reach the North Pole, explore around the ice hole through which their submarine surfaced.

Two of the *Sargo's* crew members raise the Hawaiian flag at the North Pole. Both men are natives of Hawaii.

This diagram of the USS *Skipjack* shows the general layout of a nuclear-powered submarine.

General Dynamics Corp.

Engine Room

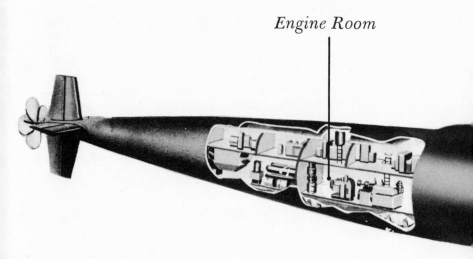

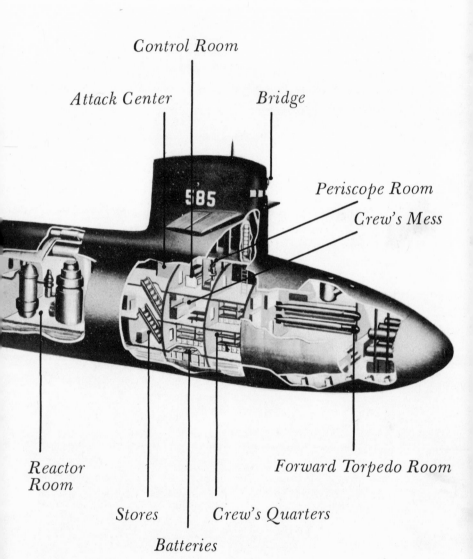

Control Room

Attack Center

Bridge

585

Periscope Room

Crew's Mess

Reactor
Room

Stores

Batteries

Crew's Quarters

Forward Torpedo Room

The *Triton*, world's largest submarine, rides the surface off the Delaware coast after her historic underwater voyage around the world.

Wide World

Deep in the heart of the *Triton*, technicians are busily at work beside the radar screens and plotting boards.

U. S. Navy

Three Soviet submarines, on an official visit to Sweden, prepare to tie up in Stockholm Harbor on June 15, 1962.

United Press

Comdr. James Osborn leans over the USS *George Washington's* bridge as the first nuclear-powered ballistic sub heads for the Atlantic.

Technicians at the center missile-level station stand by the consoles at which the Polaris missile is readied for firing. Countdown is a matter of minutes.

U. S. Navy

Missiles are loaded into the submarine through a cannister that fits over the missile-tube opening like a giant shoe horn, guiding the missile into place without a scratch.

The USS *Proteus* is one of the submarine tenders that maintain and service the fleet ballistic missile submarines, including the USS *George Washington*.

13. ATOMIC POWER GOES UNDER WATER

In 1900 the optimistic inventor John Holland said, "Larger boats [more than 200 feet long] will never be feasible unless we discover some better system of storing electricity."

But what could take the place of the batteries then in use under water? There had been some modifications of the batteries, and the Diesel engine had been adapted for submarine use. But even with these improvements and the use of the snorkel, the submarine remained a limited ship. Its power remained inadequate. Batteries weaken fast when pushing heavy objects.

Before the United States entered World War II, two engineers of the Naval Research Laboratory at Anacostia—Dr. Ross Gunn and Dr. Philipp Abelson—studied the possibility of using split-atom power to move a torpedo or submarine. Abelson drew up plans for a power plant for such a sub-

The first Polaris is launched from a submerged submarine, the *George Washington*.

marine. In 1939 they reported results to Congress. They had decided that the space was too cramped for the heavy steam plant necessary for using atomic heat. Nevertheless, a year before war broke out, they set up two experimental atomic plants, one at Anacostia under Rear Admiral Harold G. Bowen and the other at the Philadelphia shipyard under Rear Admiral T. A. Solberg.

The wartime years were devoted to gaining victory by flooding the oceans with ordinary Diesel-electric submarines. But after atomic bombs were dropped on Japan, three more Naval officers —Rear Admirals Edward L. Cochrane and Earle Mills, plus Captain Armand Morgan, all of the Bureau of Ships—demanded that a "Jules Verne submarine" be built using atomic power. Their demands were warmly backed by Secretary of the Navy James Forrestal and Chief of Naval Operations Admiral Chester Nimitz. But uranium was in short supply. The Atomic Energy Commission turned them down.

The delay ended in June, 1946, when Mills and Bowen selected a hard-driving electrical engineer to realize the dream on which Bowen had had a mere $2,000 to spend before the war. Their choice fell on Captain Hyman G. Rickover, a Navy man who had trained at the submarine school in New London. They chose well. For many years Rickover had fussed over the cranky engine and battery troubles of submarines. Every submarine had a weak heart. When Rickover, an engineer rather than a physicist, realized the tremendous amount of energy that could be obtained from the atom in the form of heat, he saw an escape from the greasy tyranny of black oil and its poisonous exhaust fumes.

The atom, when split and harnessed, was a magic fuel to banish batteries. It offered heat without using up precious oxygen by burning. An atomic-powered submarine, instead of surfacing to breathe like a seal, could stay under like a shark. The energy provided by nuclear fission could give the submarine unlimited range. Both the heavy oil tanks and the outer hull encasing them could be discarded. The atomic submarine needed only one skin, like a fish. And there would be no further need for the air-breathing snorkels, whose feathery wakes betrayed the submarines to peering enemies.

Rickover was ordered by Admirals Bowen and

Mills to report to Oak Ridge, Tennessee, with four other officers and two civilian engineers, to represent the Navy in a joint Army-Navy-civilian group effort. Their orders were to study atomic power and its possible future use for propelling vehicles, aircraft and ships. Gradually Rickover and his staff began to devote themselves to the development of a feasible working power plant for an atomic submarine. He, Mills and Bowen found ready support in Admiral Charles Styer and Lieutenant Commander Edward L. Beach, a submarine skipper. But even with such strong allies, Rickover had to fight hard to have his way. He made it a personal crusade to eliminate red tape and push the project through to an early completion. He was direct, purposeful and demanding.

Congress finally authorized the construction of a nuclear-powered vessel on July 1, 1951, and the keel was laid in June of 1952. The power plant or "reactor" used in the submarine was developed many miles from salt water at a desert site near Arco, Idaho. The Westinghouse Electric Corporation assisted in the project. The hull was built in a heavily guarded corner of the yard of the Electric Boat Company at Groton, Connecticut.

(The company is now the Electric Boat Division of General Dynamics Corporation.)

On January 21, 1954, Mrs. Dwight Eisenhower broke the traditional bottle of champagne on the submarine's bow as the boat slid down the ways into the Thames River. "I christen thee United States Ship *Nautilus*," she said.

The age of the true submersible had begun.

The secret of the *Nautilus'* remarkable nuclear power plant lies in her reactor. The fuel for the reactor is a core of radioactive uranium. Its atoms constantly give off particles called neutrons. When a neutron from one atom strikes another atom, the second atom splits. This break, called "fission," releases a tremendous amount of energy in the form of heat. It releases additional neutrons as well, and these strike still more atoms, splitting them. Thus more heat and more neutrons are released. A chain reaction is set up.

This reaction can be slowed down by inserting into the core several rods made of a metal that absorbs neutrons. If the rods are withdrawn part way, the speed of the reaction increases again.

The submarine's reactor is designed so that the reaction can never lead to an atomic explosion.

Of course an enormous amount of heat is released by the fission or breaking up of the uranium atoms. This heat is absorbed by water circulating around the core in a closed and shielded loop. The so-called primary water is kept under high pressure to prevent it from turning into steam. Flowing through heat exchangers, the water transfers its heat to a secondary water system, but without passing on any radioactivity from the nuclear core.

The water in the secondary system boils into steam. This steam drives the ship's propulsion turbines. The turbines turn the ship's propellers. The same steam also drives generators to charge batteries which provide power for lighting, air-conditioning and other auxiliary motors.

The *Nautilus* was not cheap to build. A 312-foot fleet submarine cost about ten million dollars, whereas the atomic newcomer—only eight feet longer—cost forty million dollars for the boat's hull stripped. Then there was another fifteen million for the reactor.

At 11:00 A.M. on January 17, 1955, Commander

Eugene P. Wilkinson flashed from the bridge of *Nautilus* his historic announcement: "Underway on nuclear power." On a shakedown cruise from New London, Connecticut, to San Juan, Puerto Rico, *Nautilus* ran 1,300 miles submerged in just 84 hours.

Earlier American submarines, using batteries, had never been able to cruise more than an hour submerged at their top underwater speed of nine to twelve knots. Yet *Nautilus*, tirelessly propelled by her slaving atoms, ran hour after hour at sixteen to twenty knots. She sped 3,100 miles in 200 hours. Rickover was pleased, but not surprised. "*Nautilus* has been designed to operate better and faster under water than on the surface," he said. "Our aim is to design nuclear propulsion plants which can last for an entire war without being refueled."

An inexhaustible submarine, Rickover argued, could "stay well within the enemy's borders and keep the battlefield away from the United States." When the new submarine launched rockets or missiles, it could "keep its launching position undisclosed."

The *Nautilus'* greatest mission was a daring ex-

ploratory voyage through the hidden seas under
the polar icecap. She was the second United
States submarine—and the second *Nautilus*—to
attempt to penetrate the arctic underwater regions.
In 1931 Sir Hubert Wilkins, an Australian ex-
plorer, tried to take the overage American submarine *0-12*, renamed *Nautilus*, under the icecap.
She set out bravely, carrying divers trained for
polar seas and special saws to cut through ice
for air holes. At the edge of the ice pack, however, her worn-out diving fins fell off. Wilkins
managed to get her nose down far enough to
slide under the ice pack a few times. But when
frost formed on the machinery, the attempt was
abandoned.

Later, the American submarines *Boarfish* and
Carp made explorations of a few miles under ice.
They developed an upside-down fathometer, or
depth measurer, that could be used to bounce
signals off the roof of ice.

But still the big questions remained. How could
a submarine find a breathing hole through the
ice? Would it be caught under the arctic icecap
like a fly in a refrigerator, imprisoned forever in
an ice cube?

Equipped with five fathometers designed by physicist Waldo K. Lyon, the new *Nautilus* set out. She had special compasses to counteract the dizzying spin of the magnetic pole. And her new skipper was Commander William R. Anderson, who took along twenty-five torpedoes to blow a hole in the ice, if necessary.

Anderson started off with a record trip of 150 miles under Atlantic pack ice. But coming up in an "arctic lagoon,"—one of many holes in the icecap—he smashed both periscopes. In another stab at the Pole from the Atlantic side, *Nautilus* stayed three days below the ice. But then her compasses, unused to the freak magnetism of the true and magnetic poles, began playing what the sailors called "longitude roulette." They were spinning like a gambler's wheel. The *Nautilus* finally broke into clear water again off Greenland.

With the consent of President Dwight D. Eisenhower, the Navy decided to make a second, secret try from the direction of the Pacific, through the Bering Sea. Here the icy curtain hangs down from the surface almost to the bottom, and the water is only 120 feet deep in places. It would be a tight squeeze at first for

Nautilus to creep under, but better than coming from the Atlantic direction and being trapped on the polar side of the ice curtain.

To insure secrecy, the number of the *Nautilus*, 571, was painted out before she left Puget Sound in Washington. Then Anderson took his microphone: "All hands, this is the captain speaking. Our destination for this trip is Portland, England, via the North Pole." A shiver of pride, slightly chilled with nervousness, ran through the boat.

At first *Nautilus*, trying the western passage of the Bering Strait, was blocked by deep ice off the Siberian coastline. The wall here hung sixty feet below the motionless, frozen surface. Anderson backed away and tried the eastern gate. It was a little better. But the sub's "ice pick," the spiky radio antenna, was only twenty feet from the roof, and her propellers were only forty feet off the bottom.

Soon the submarine found herself wedged in a place where the hard bottom and icy roof gave her only five feet of clearance in which to continue. Reluctantly Anderson crept out, pushed up his antennas and flashed Pearl Harbor that he had failed.

After planes had scouted the frozen eaves of the

arctic roof for an opening, *Nautilus* again pointed her bow north. Late in July she squeezed through the "brash and block" ice off the Alaskan coast, passed the Bering Strait, and met the dirty black ice of the Chuckchi Sea. Blocked again, she crept eastward along the Alaskan shore. Soon she reached the subway of the Arctic, the long under-water tunnel that leads north from Point Barrow. A school of walruses followed her, but they were disappointed when her underwater slot for dumping garbage broke, cutting off their meals.

For the remaining 1,094 miles to the Pole the roof of ice over the *Nautilus* averaged only twenty feet thick. Some upside-down bergs, however, ran down as far as sixty-five feet. But the ocean floor was more than a mile below. *Nautilus* swam north at a fast twenty knots. Her course was easy for the helmsman to remember: zero-zero-zero, or "true north." No sweaters were needed, however, for it was seventy-two degrees throughout the boat. Could the men really be so comfortable 200 feet under the frozen waste?

After sixty-two hours the *Nautilus* and her crew drew near the Pole. Anderson stepped to the microphone and said:

"The distance to the Pole is now precisely

four-tenths of a mile. As we approach, let us pause in silence, dedicated in thanks for the blessings that have been ours during this remarkable voyage. Let our prayers be for lasting world peace and in solemn tribute to those who have preceded us, whether in victory or defeat."

The 116 officers, experts and sailors fell silent. Only the pinging of the sonar could be heard, reaching out for the icy roof 400 feet above. Then Anderson, watching the hand of the indicator, said: "Stand by . . . ten seconds . . . eight . . . six . . . four . . . three . . . two . . . Mark! August 3, 1958. Time 23:15. For the United States and the United States Navy, the North Pole." A cheer ran through the narrow passages as *Nautilus* plowed on, over the top of the world, and "downhill" toward home.

For two days *Nautilus* ran south toward the Atlantic, looking for a hole. The sailors were already writing letters to their families before she found an opening in the ice big enough to permit her to emerge. Then the crew raised the "port whip," and radioed the magic message, "*Nautilus* 90 North."

Nautilus ran her first 62,500 miles on a single core of uranium. The power she used, according

to Rickover, was equal to 2,170,000 gallons of
Diesel oil. But she was costly. The uranium,
despite Rickover's skill as a penny pincher, cost
four million dollars—twenty times as much as oil!

But this huge investment quickly brought returns
in many fields of knowledge. More was learned
about the effects of long emersion. Jack L. Kinsey,
medical officer aboard the *Nautilus*, found that the
condition of the men depended partly on what
kind of electrical charges, called "air ions," were
released in the boat. If the air-borne charges
were positive, he found they caused "depressed
feelings, irritability, fatigue, headaches and dizzi-
ness." But if the ions had a minus charge, they
caused "optimism, exhilaration, relief of asthma
and hay fever, a drop in pulse rate and blood
pressure, increased growth rate and more rapid
healing of wounds and burns."

Only four months after news of the triumph of
the *Nautilus* spread throughout the world, Sir
Hubert Wilkins, the first arctic submarine ex-
plorer, died. His last wish was that his ashes be
taken by submarine to the North Pole. *Skate*, the
third nuclear sub to come off the assembly line,
was selected for the mission. She was just 265
feet long and weighed only two-thirds as much as

Nautilus. This time word came through fast: "*Skate* is on the surface at the North Pole." And the crew reported they had met their pledge, "scattering his [Wilkins'] ashes into the blowing snow."

The Navy had now committed itself to the atomic submarine. New ships were launched at a surprisingly rapid pace. The United States soon had a fleet of them: *Skipjack*, *Swordfish*, *Sargo* and *Seadragon*, in addition to the *Skate* and *Nautilus*. The model for their hull was a Diesel-electric submarine, the *Albacore*, the Navy's first high-speed submarine. It had been given a body that was streamlined and snout-nosed, like a whale or blimp. Later, these hulls were slimmed down as a result of tests in wind tunnels.

The atomic submarines are practically able to "fly" below the waves, but their maximum speed is a secret. They go so fast, in fact, that the Navy has installed airplane-type controls in place of the old-fashioned steering wheel and depth controls.

With the *Triton*, the United States Navy launched the biggest, most powerful submarine yet made—an underwater cruiser that cost more than one hundred million dollars. She displaces 5,700 tons empty; 8,000 tons when full and submerged. She is equal to the weight of four destroyers! She contains two nuclear power plants and stretches out to a length equaling that of one and a half football fields.

Triton is classified as a "radar picket," a post World War II assignment for submarines. Her job is to lie off enemy waters far ahead of a task force to give early warning of approaching ships and aircraft. She can also trace an enemy's missiles as they pass overhead. *Triton* tested her two reactors by retracing Magellan's route around the world—36,104 miles in 84 days, submerged all the way.

Vice Admiral Rickover, who had finally received a promotion in recognition of his fine job, wanted atomic submarines to be kept at sea almost continuously. He recommended rest periods for alternate crews. He wanted more submarines, he said, "many of them hiding under the polar icecap. They would constitute a fleet-in-being, ready for immediate use at any time."

Were these new nuclear submarines supposed to sink enemy ships? No, the submarine of the future would be able to strike far inland. Instead of torpedoes it would use rockets. Instead of sending its spears through the sea, it would throw them through the air.

The idea was not new. In 1942, during World War II, the Germans had fired a missile from a submarine submerged in ninety-six feet of water at their secret experimental base. They were prevented from sending submarines to strike the American cities only by some of their high-ranking officers who didn't believe the missiles could be aimed well or cause great damage.

After the war the German rocket experts, led by Wernher von Braun, explained that they had fired more than twenty such missiles from below the sea. In 1955, the year *Nautilus* was launched, Rear Admiral William F. Raborn decided that it was time to give the missile a chance to be fired from the swaying deck of a submarine on the surface and from the stable hull of a submarine deep in the quiet depths. Atomic warheads would make it possible for submarines to destroy cities.

The giant intercontinental missiles already developed for firing from land bases used a liquid fuel. They were too dangerous to keep in a submarine because of their dangerous gases. They were also too big. The Navy was searching for a missile that used a solid fuel in a cartridge small enough to fit neatly into a submarine's hull.

The first missile to be carried by American submarines—for firing only when surfaced—was the Regulus. It could be used against targets more than 500 miles from the launching ship. And it was able to carry either an atomic warhead or conventional high explosives. Submariners, however, like to shoot from below the waves, where they feel safest. Soon Admiral Raborn gave them the new missile Polaris, named for the North Star. Polaris is nearly 30 feet long and weighs 30,000 pounds. A new submarine had to be designed to carry the mammoth weapon.

Polaris burns a solid fuel. It can be safely stored in a submarine, and it carries a nuclear warhead. When the submarine is under water, the missile can be fired up through the waves by a great push of compressed air, just like its ancestor, the torpedo. On July 20, 1960, the first Polaris was fired off Cape Canaveral from the submerged *George Washington*, one of the new missile-bearing nuclear subs.

Soon more of these hundred-million-dollar missile submarines appeared—*Patrick Henry*, *Abraham Lincoln*, *Robert E. Lee*, *Theodore Roosevelt*, and others.

Each can carry sixteen gray-green missiles. Instead of lying lengthwise like torpedoes, the missiles point up at the skies. The Navy plans included at least forty-five Polaris submarines.

The missile submarine has overtaken the fading heavy bomber. It has become the most powerful weapon in the world directly guided by a human crew. The submarine, originally intended only to strike floating ships, can now strike at—and even wipe out—great cities hundreds of miles from the sea. Once the Polaris leaps from below the waves, it can fly 1,400 miles in 17 minutes. Its real job, however, is not to destroy the enemy but to discourage him from attacking.

But how are America's cities—many of them easy coastal targets—to be defended against enemy missile submarines lying perhaps in mid-Atlantic waters? As a solution to that problem, the Navy has developed a class of submarine designed chiefly for anti-submarine warfare. The *Tullibee*, launched in 1960, is the first of these.

Meanwhile, the ice-bound seas of the North have also been explored further. *Skate* made two crossings under the arctic ice between the Pacific and Atlantic, in both summer and winter. On March 17, 1959, she surfaced at the North Pole and planted her flag where Admiral Robert E. Peary had gone by dogteam almost exactly fifty years before, on April 6, 1909. Since 1959 other nuclear subs have traveled under the arctic icecap.

New submarine ideas spread all over the world. The Soviets, already owners of a huge fleet of Diesel submarines, made arrangements for their working all over the world with radar-equipped "fishing boats" as spying scouts. Soon they announced that they had atomic subs, too. Britain borrowed American designs and began her first atomic submarine, the *Dreadnaught*.

But the atomic submarines were not perfect. The United States Navy found that their speed made them noisy. To quiet the telltale rush of water along their hulls, the Navy has been studying the dolphin, the symbol of the submariners. Scientist and engineers have found that the dolphin has a yielding skin. This skin gives slightly when the dolphin swims fast, without making its prey aware that it is coming. A similar skin has been adapted for use by the atomic submarines.

To get away from the watery noises, the Navy also experimented with smaller submarines operating on "fuel cells." This is a kind of chemical battery that creates its own electrical reaction. It is far ahead of the old batteries that had to be charged. Submarines powered by these fuel cells have not been able to go as far as the atomic monsters, but they are cheaper.

The Navy has also experimented with automatic guidance machines as another way of cutting down costs of nuclear subs. These electrical brains have been designed to reduce the crews from 120 men to 12.

Though America, during the 1960s, established herself as the world's leading undersea power, her submarine officers still kept in mind that many of the basic ideas they used were born in other countries. They also remembered that neither they nor any other nation has ever conquered the sea.

In several of the atomic submarines, screwed in a corner of the captain's desk, is a little brass plate with an inscription. Such an inscription and plate were first placed on *Skipjack* by a New London neighbor of the captain, W. W. Behrens.

The brass plate bears words from a hymn sung by French fishermen. They are words all sub-mariners often repeat in their hearts:

"O God, Thy sea is so vast and my boat is so small."

INDEX